MW00575850

The Whiz Kids from D.A.R.P.A.

Book One

Ramon Gil
Stories & Art

David Kawalec
Editing

Macareña Cortez
Color Assistance

Emilio Villajuan-Gil
Research Assistance

Read the webcomic

StoryArk Press

Table of Contents

Please direct all inquiries to ramonsgil@gmail.com.

Introduction

Ever since I was a child, I've always been curious about things. I would figure out how things like gears, propellers and carjacks worked. I was fascinated by UFOs, pyramids and the Bermuda Triangle. I loved science fiction and spy movies and documentaries. And I loved, loved, LOVED reading comic books.

What you hold in your hand is me trying to combine everything I love into one experience. And not just about the topics I already mentioned, but about ideas, dreams and outlooks on life. About love and relationships, how to be a contributing member of society and how to be happy. Basically, I'm hoping this book and future ones will let me explore and discuss, with you the reader, all the thoughts and things that are swirling in my head.

"It requires a very unusual mind to undertake the analysis of the obvious."
— Alfred North Whitehead

This is a motto I've lived with all my life and I don't care how crazy it sounds. It keeps life interesting.

Anyway, this book is also about fun and laughter as well as scientific discovery. I hope you enjoy reading it as much as I've enjoyed making it. And I truly hope it sparks scientific curiosity in you.

Ramon Gil

Chapter One:

Brain Freeze

While touring a new underground facility,
disaster strikes forcing the Whiz Kids
to spring into action!

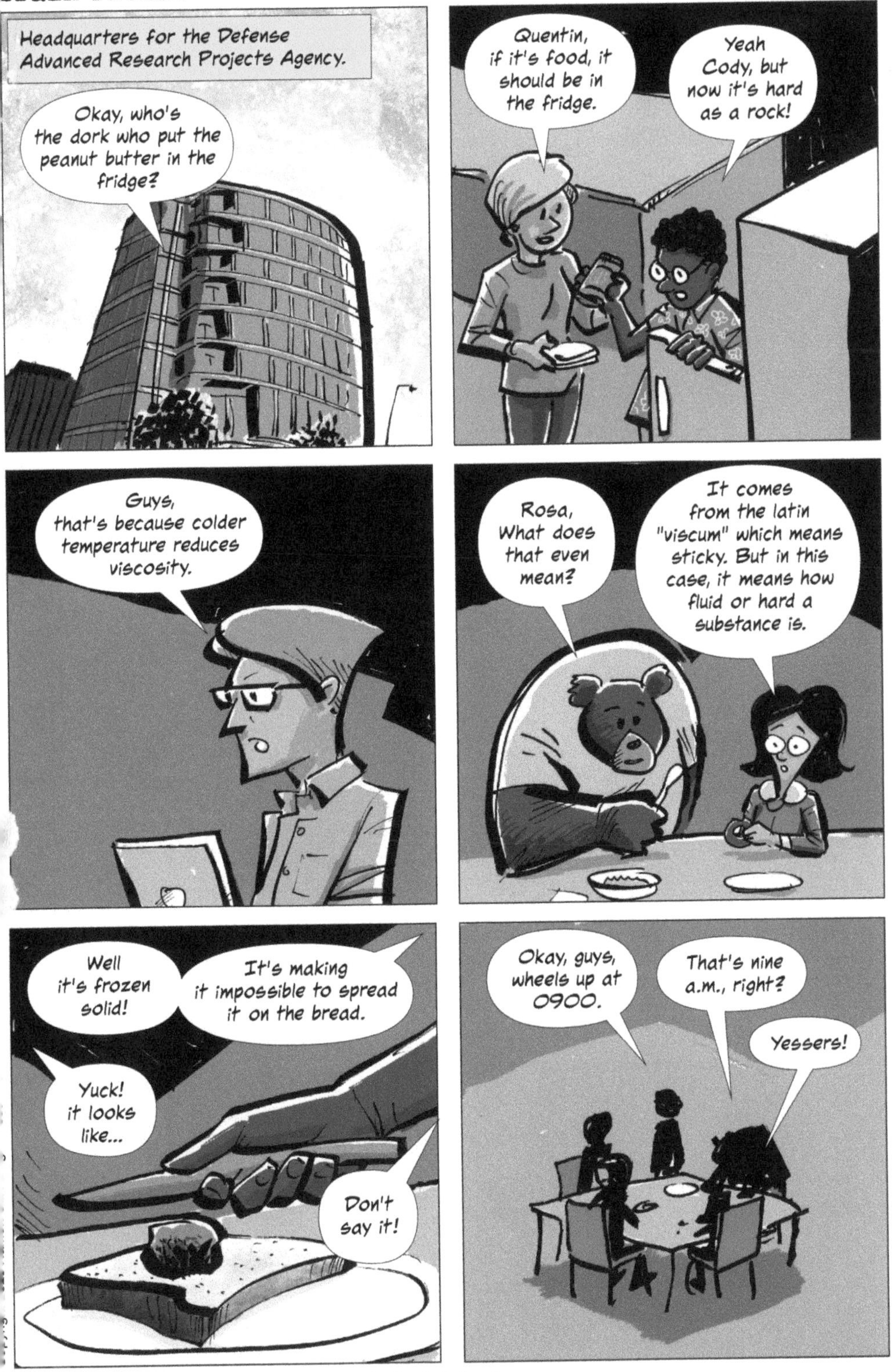
Headquarters for the Defense Advanced Research Projects Agency.
Okay, who's the dork who put the peanut butter in the fridge?
Quentin, if it's food, it should be in the fridge.
Yeah Cody, but now it's hard as a rock!
Guys, that's because colder temperature reduces viscosity.
Rosa, What does that even mean?
It comes from the latin "viscum" which means sticky. But in this case, it means how fluid or hard a substance is.
Well it's frozen solid!
It's making it impossible to spread it on the bread.
Yuck! it looks like...
Don't say it!
Okay, guys, wheels up at 0900.
That's nine a.m., right?
Yessers!

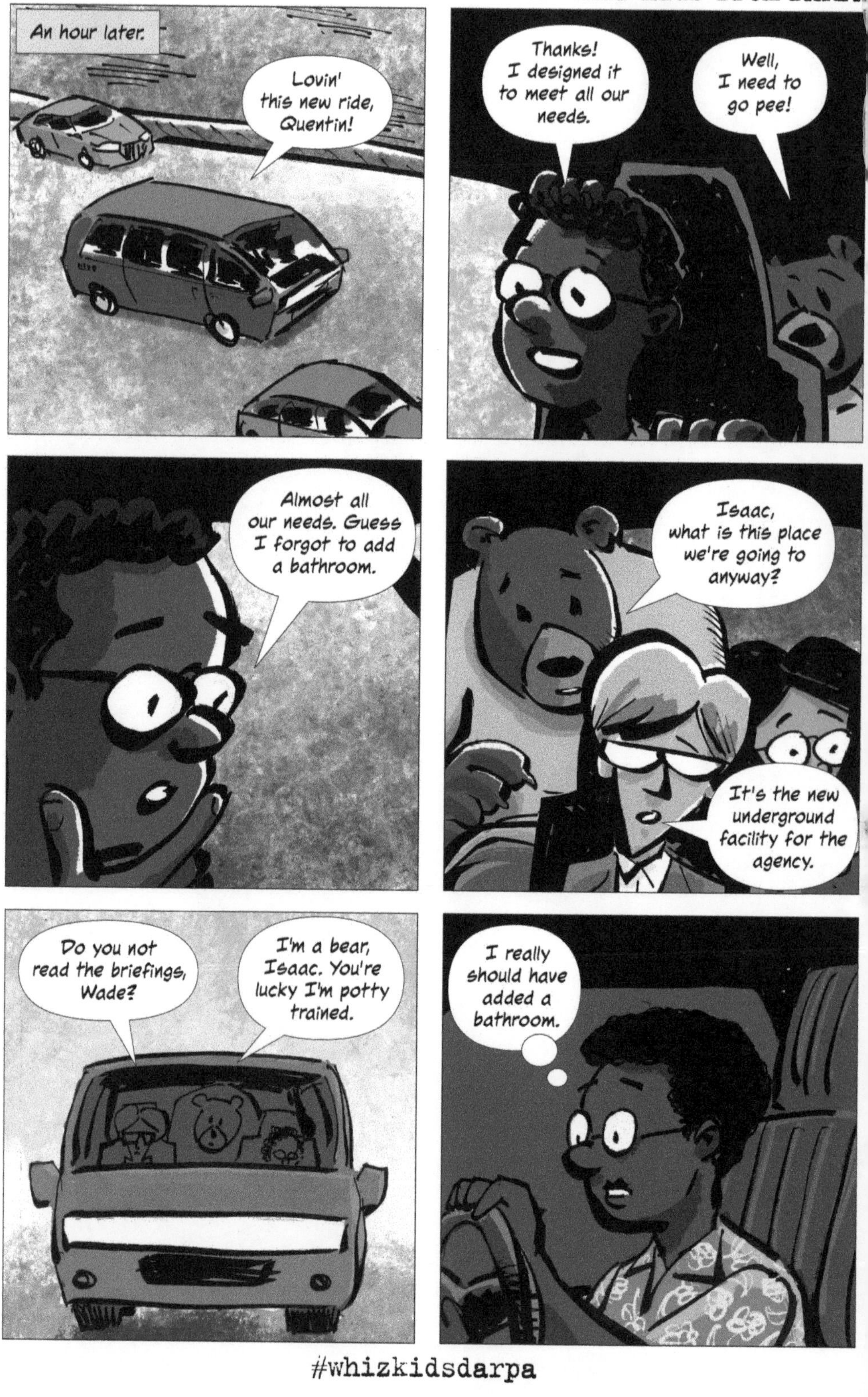
An hour later.
Lovin' this new ride, Quentin!
Thanks! I designed it to meet all our needs.
Well, I need to go pee!
Almost all our needs. Guess I forgot to add a bathroom.
Isaac, what is this place we're going to anyway?
It's the new underground facility for the agency.
Do you not read the briefings, Wade?
I'm a bear, Isaac. You're lucky I'm potty trained.
I really should have added a bathroom.

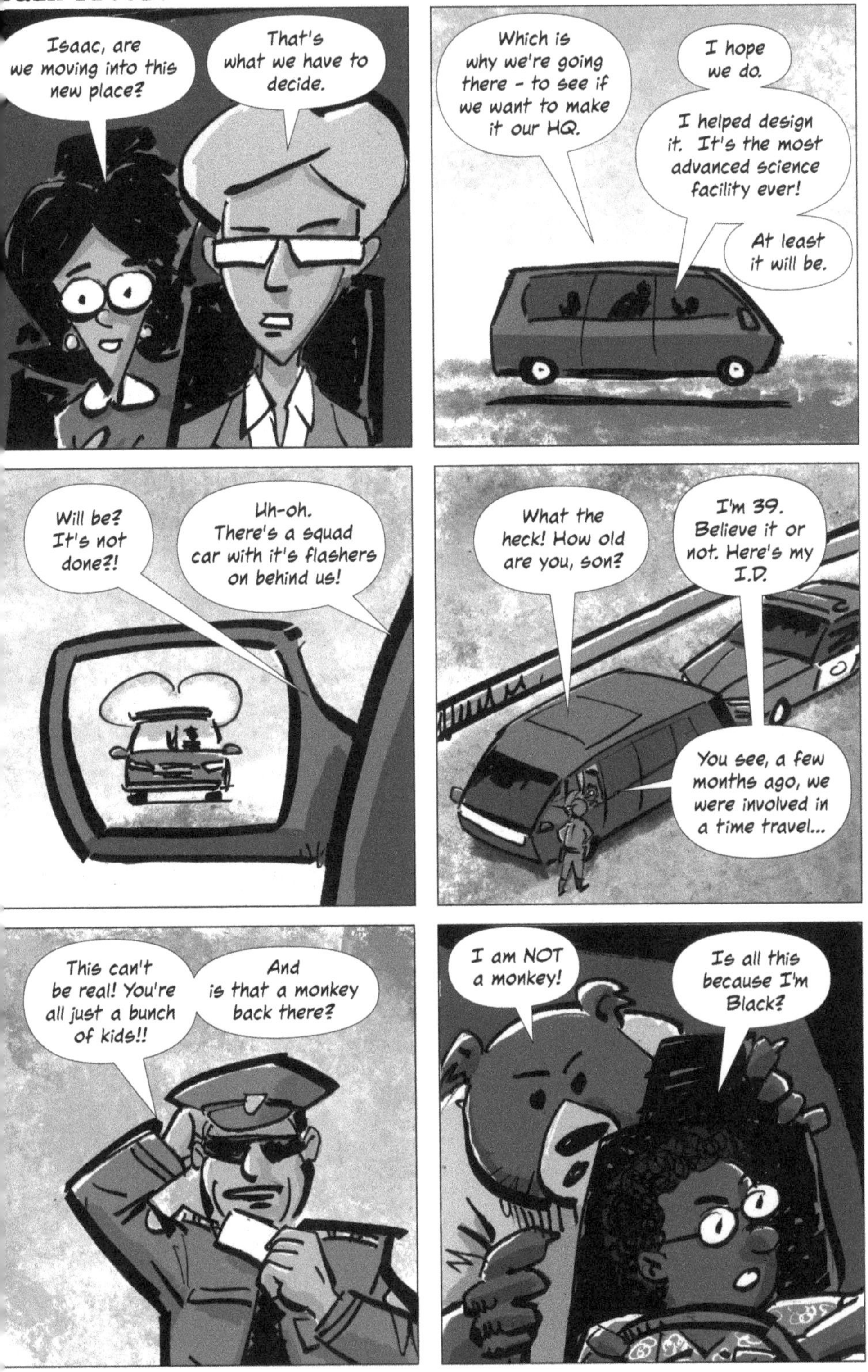
Isaac, are we moving into this new place?
That's what we have to decide.
Which is why we're going there - to see if we want to make it our HQ.
I hope we do.
I helped design it. It's the most advanced science facility ever!
At least it will be.
Will be? It's not done?!
Uh-oh. There's a squad car with it's flashers on behind us!
What the heck! How old are you, son?
I'm 39. Believe it or not. Here's my I.D.
You see, a few months ago, we were involved in a time travel...
This can't be real! You're all just a bunch of kids!!
And is that a monkey back there?
I am NOT a monkey!
Is all this because I'm Black?

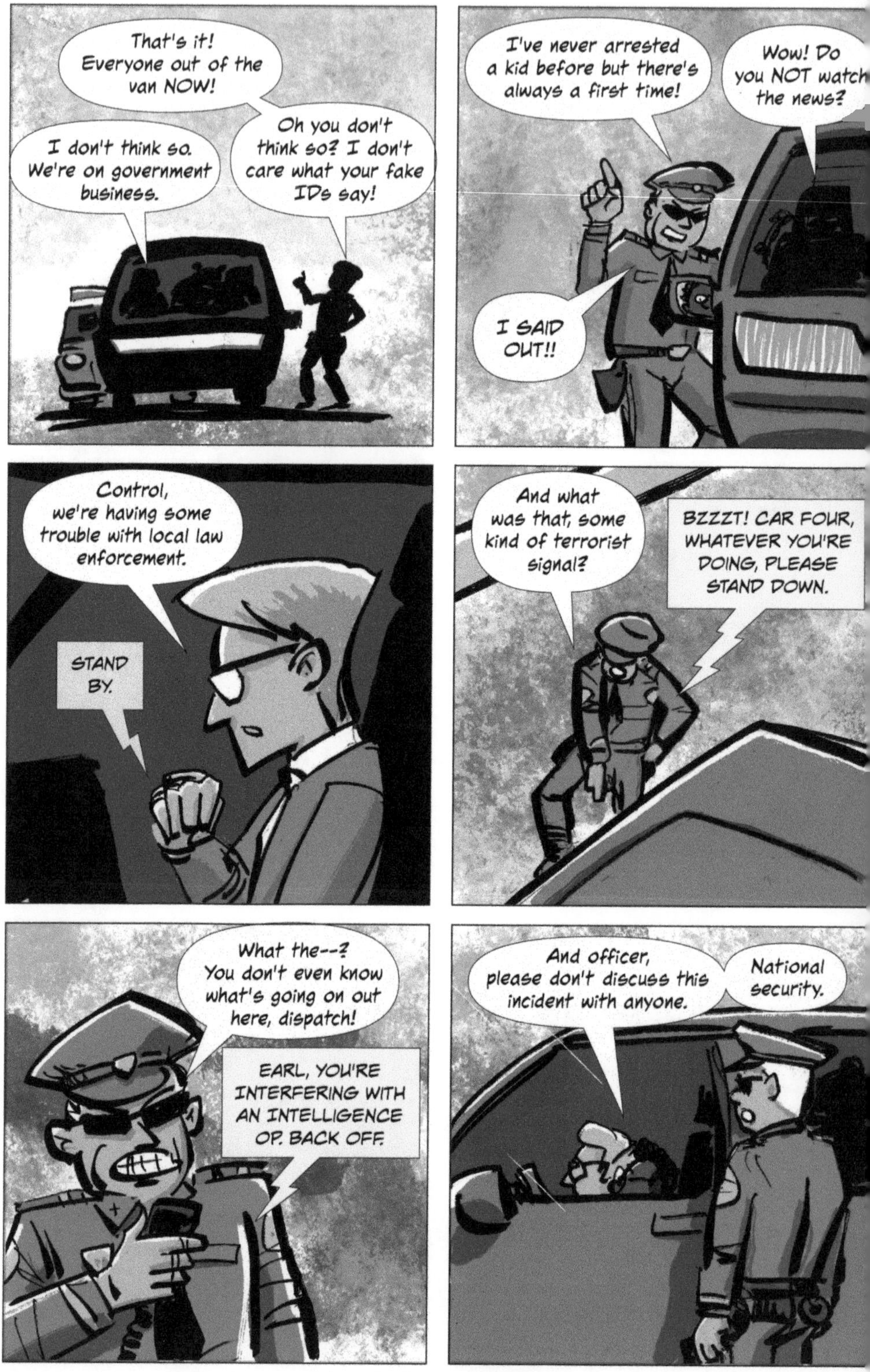
That's it! Everyone out of the van NOW!
I don't think so. We're on government business.
Oh you don't think so? I don't care what your fake IDs say!
I've never arrested a kid before but there's always a first time!
Wow! Do you NOT watch the news?
I SAID OUT!!
Control, we're having some trouble with local law enforcement.
STAND BY.
And what was that, some kind of terrorist signal?
BZZZT! CAR FOUR, WHATEVER YOU'RE DOING, PLEASE STAND DOWN.
What the--? You don't even know what's going on out here, dispatch!
EARL, YOU'RE INTERFERING WITH AN INTELLIGENCE OP. BACK OFF.
And officer, please don't discuss this incident with anyone.
National security.

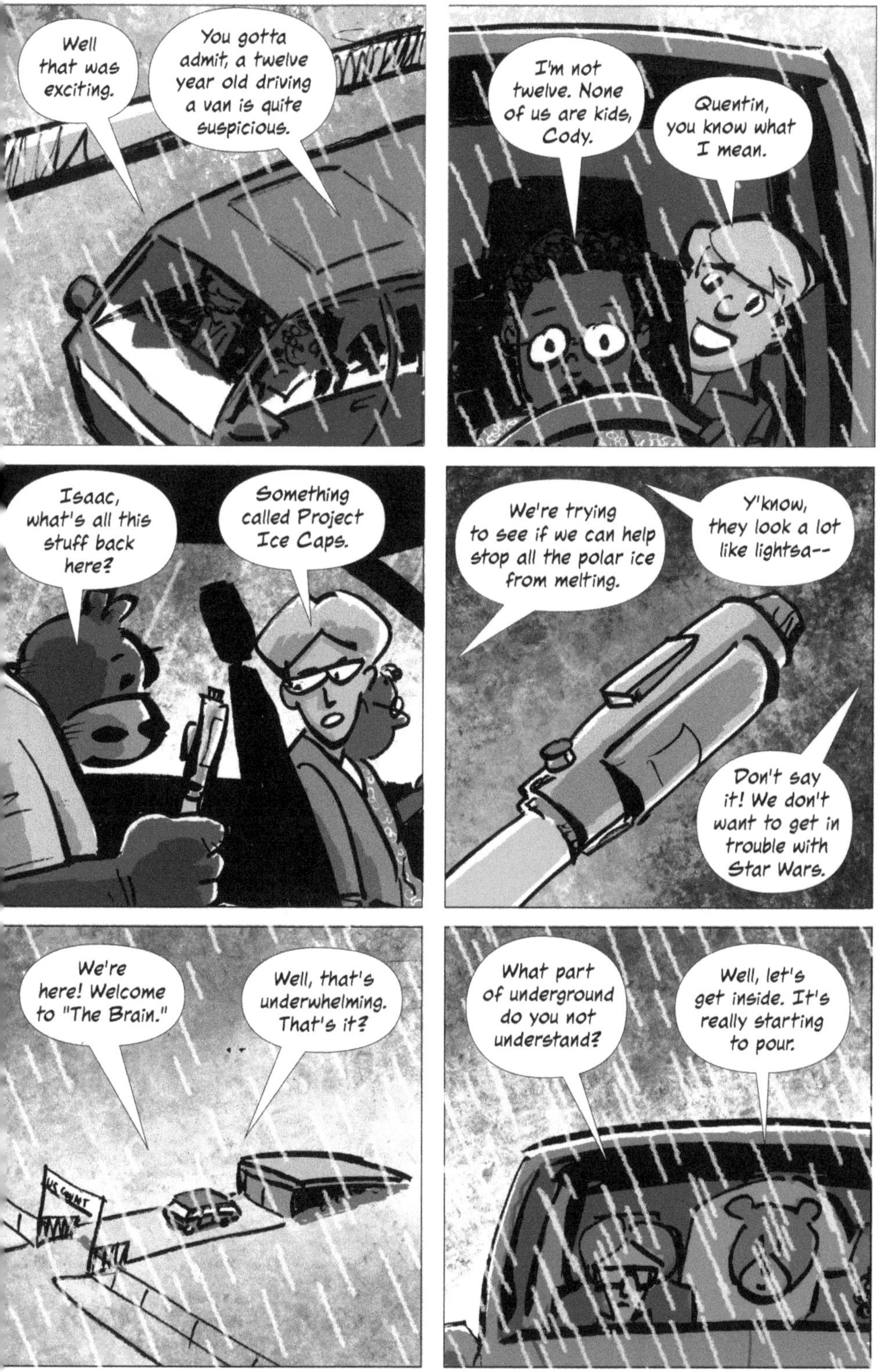
Well that was exciting.
You gotta admit, a twelve year old driving a van is quite suspicious.
I'm not twelve. None of us are kids, Cody.
Quentin, you know what I mean.
Isaac, what's all this stuff back here?
Something called Project Ice Caps.
We're trying to see if we can help stop all the polar ice from melting.
Y'know, they look a lot like lightsa--
Don't say it! We don't want to get in trouble with Star Wars.
We're here! Welcome to "The Brain."
Well, that's underwhelming. That's it?
What part of underground do you not understand?
Well, let's get inside. It's really starting to pour.

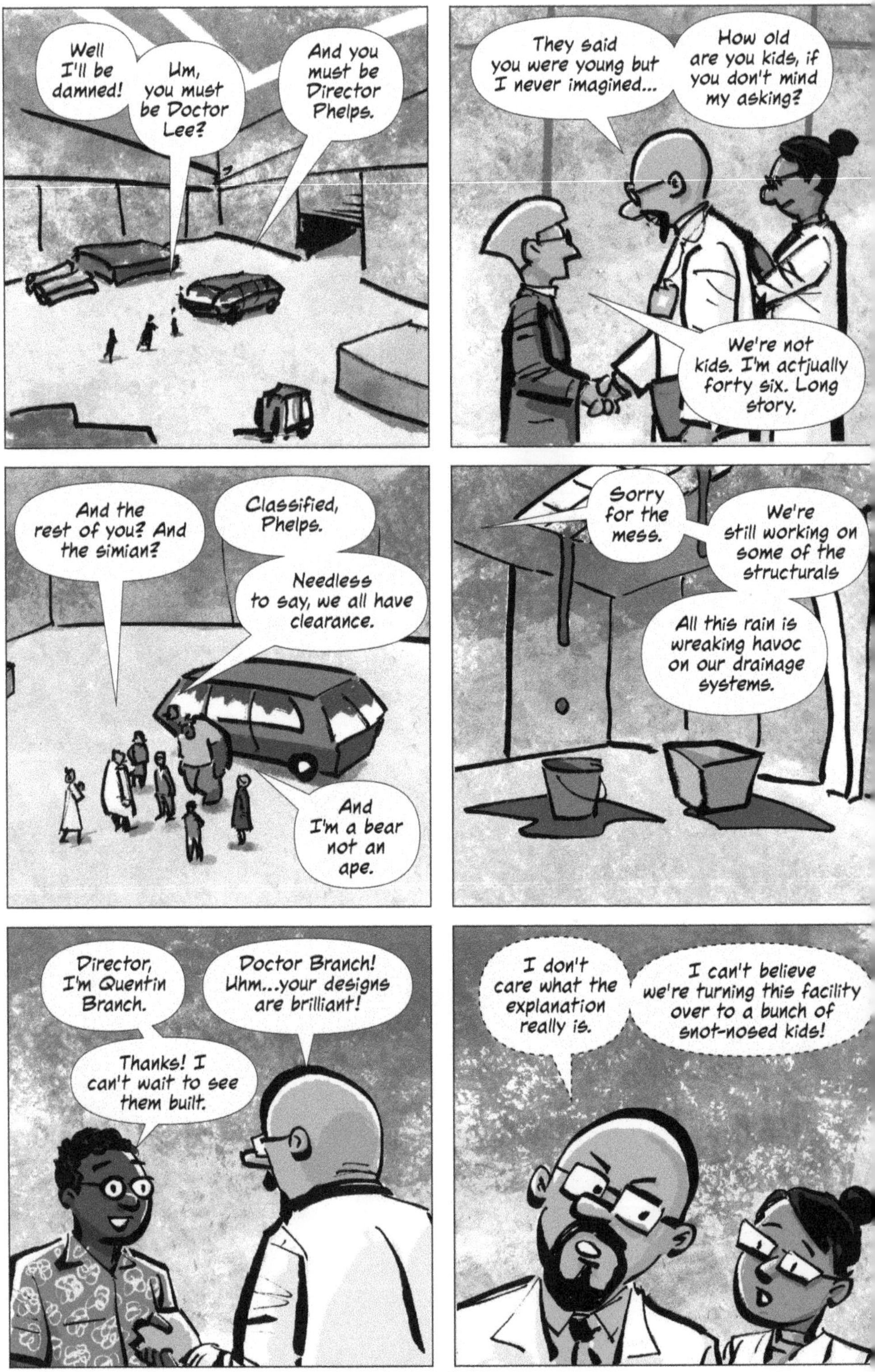
Well I'll be damned!
Um, you must be Doctor Lee?
And you must be Director Phelps.
They said you were young but I never imagined...
How old are you kids, if you don't mind my asking?
We're not kids. I'm actjually forty six. Long story.
And the rest of you? And the simian?
Classified, Phelps.
Needless to say, we all have clearance.
And I'm a bear not an ape.
Sorry for the mess.
We're still working on some of the structurals
All this rain is wreaking havoc on our drainage systems.
Director, I'm Quentin Branch.
Doctor Branch! Uhm...your designs are brilliant!
Thanks! I can't wait to see them built.
I don't care what the explanation really is.
I can't believe we're turning this facility over to a bunch of snot-nosed kids!

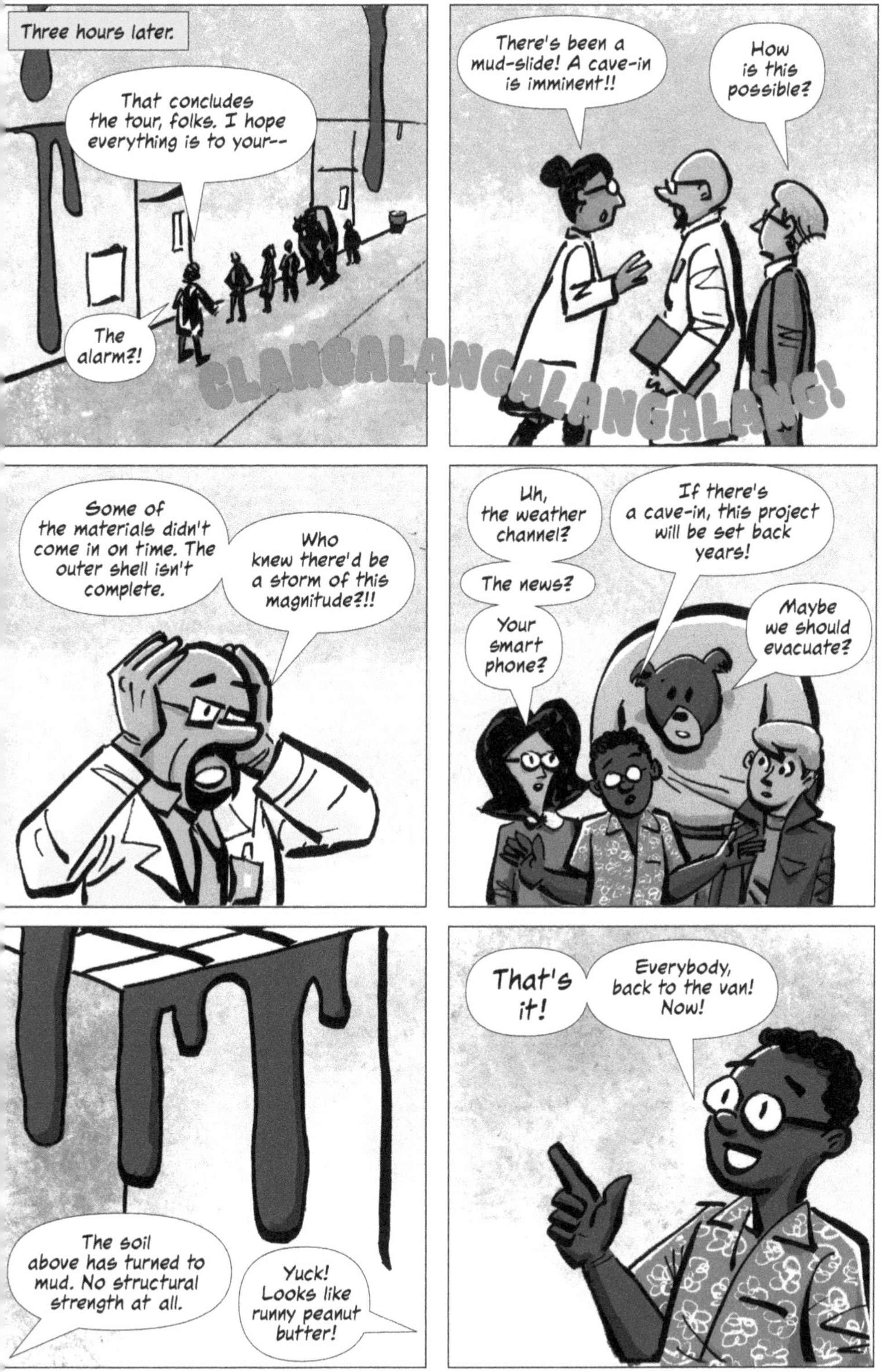
Three hours later.
That concludes the tour, folks. I hope everything is to your--
The alarm?!
There's been a mud-slide! A cave-in is imminent!!
How is this possible?
CLANGALANGALANGALANGALANG!
Some of the materials didn't come in on time. The outer shell isn't complete.
Who knew there'd be a storm of this magnitude?!!
Uh, the weather channel?
The news?
Your smart phone?
If there's a cave-in, this project will be set back years!
Maybe we should evacuate?
The soil above has turned to mud. No structural strength at all.
Yuck! Looks like runny peanut butter!
That's it!
Everybody, back to the van! Now!

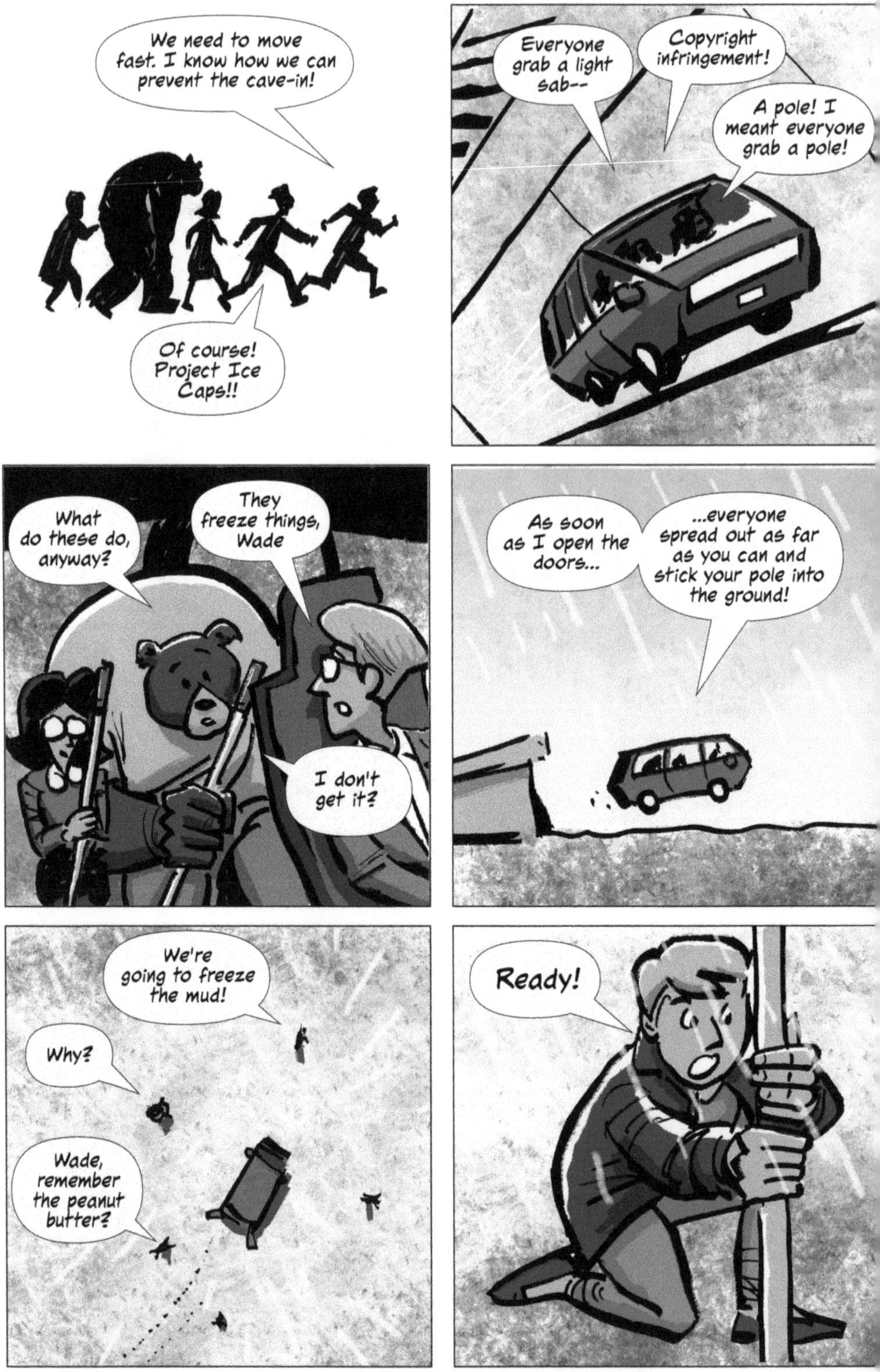
We need to move fast. I know how we can prevent the cave-in!
Of course! Project Ice Caps!!
Everyone grab a light sab--
Copyright infringement!
A pole! I meant everyone grab a pole!
What do these do, anyway?
They freeze things, Wade
I don't get it?
As soon as I open the doors...
...everyone spread out as far as you can and stick your pole into the ground!
We're going to freeze the mud!
Why?
Wade, remember the peanut butter?
Ready!

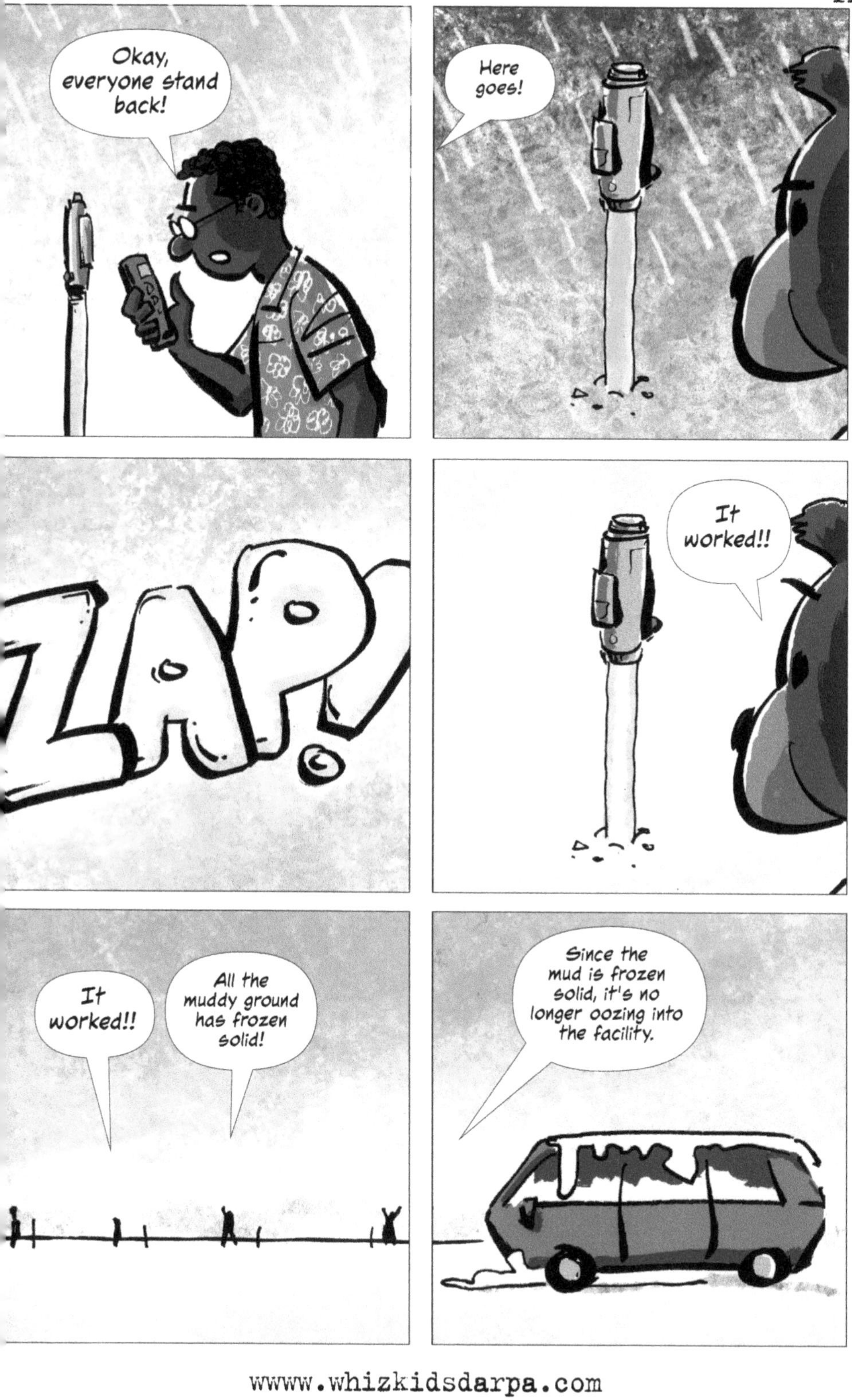
Okay, everyone stand back!
Here goes!
ZAP!
It worked!!
It worked!!
All the muddy ground has frozen solid!
Since the mud is frozen solid, it's no longer oozing into the facility.

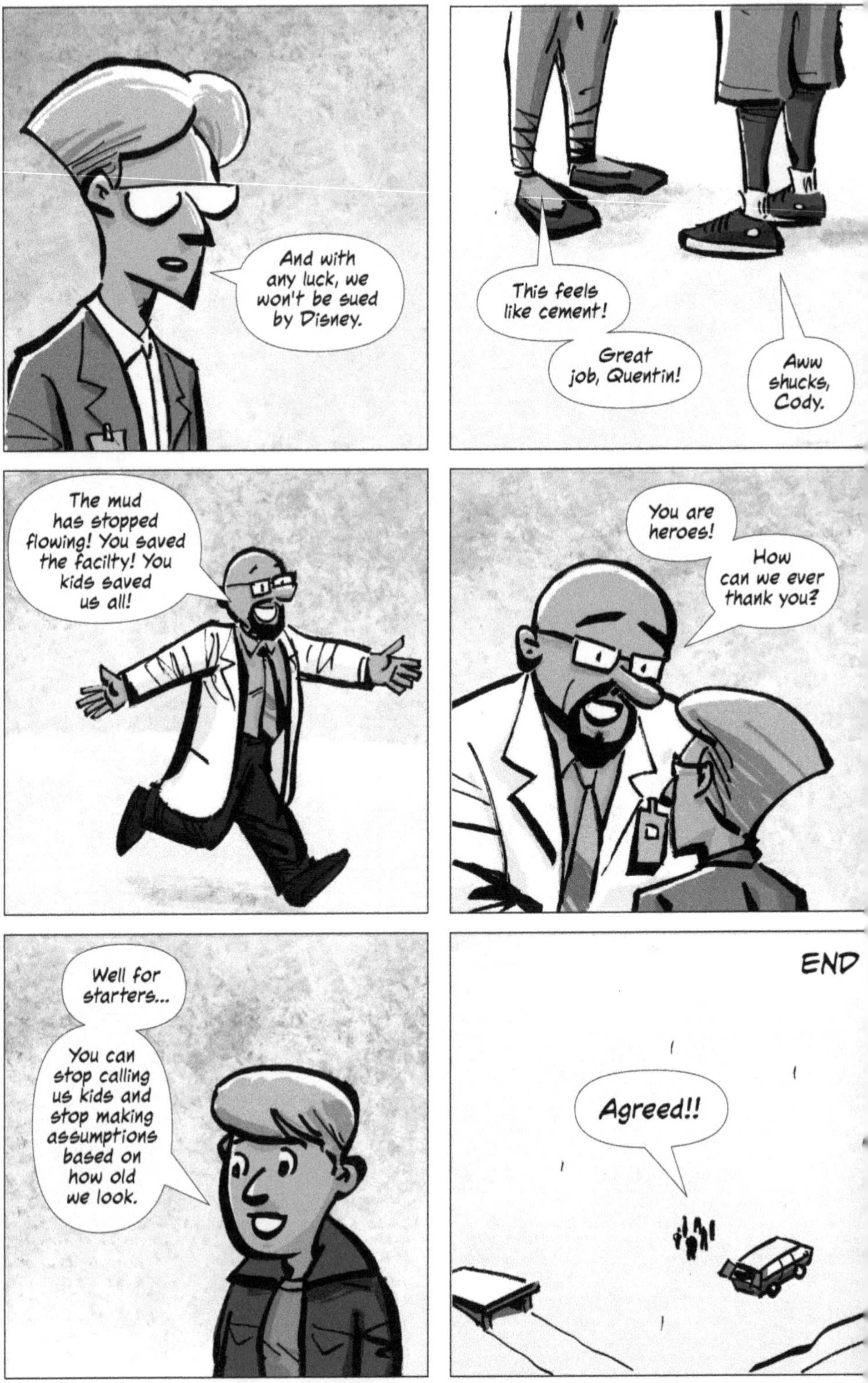
And with any luck, we won't be sued by Disney.
This feels like cement!
Great job, Quentin!
Aww shucks, Cody.
The mud has stopped flowing! You saved the facilty! You kids saved us all!
You are heroes!
How can we ever thank you?
Well for starters...
You can stop calling us kids and stop making assumptions based on how old we look.
END
Agreed!!

Science Check

Ground Freezing

This is a method of strengthening and stabilizing large areas of soil during construction and excavations to prevent collapse in tunnels and other underground structures. A freezing device (usually pipes) is embedded into the ground and refrigerants are run through them which freezes the surrounding soil making it as hard as cement. Ground freezing can also be used to prevent toxic contaminants in soil from leaking or spreading.

For more information:
http://www.whizkidsdarpa.com/groundfreezing

Chapter Two:
Isaac's Story

We learn a little about Isaac and why he
is such a loyal supporter and defender of those
who need help most.

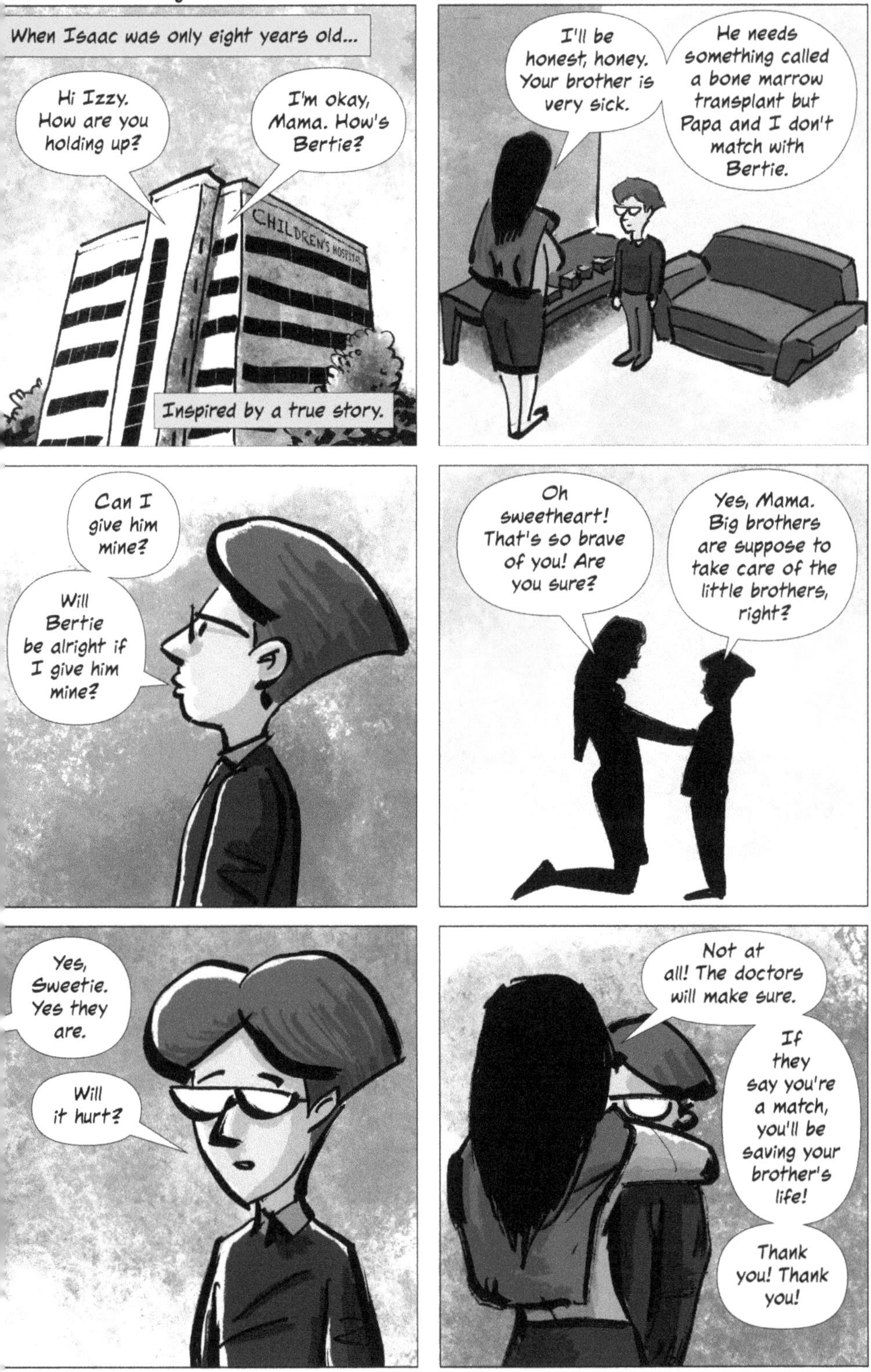
When Isaac was only eight years old...
Hi Izzy. How are you holding up?
I'm okay, Mama. How's Bertie?
CHILDREN'S HOSPITAL
Inspired by a true story.
I'll be honest, honey. Your brother is very sick.
He needs something called a bone marrow transplant but Papa and I don't match with Bertie.
Can I give him mine?
Will Bertie be alright if I give him mine?
Oh sweetheart! That's so brave of you! Are you sure?
Yes, Mama. Big brothers are suppose to take care of the little brothers, right?
Yes, Sweetie. Yes they are.
Will it hurt?
Not at all! The doctors will make sure.
If they say you're a match, you'll be saving your brother's life!
Thank you! Thank you!

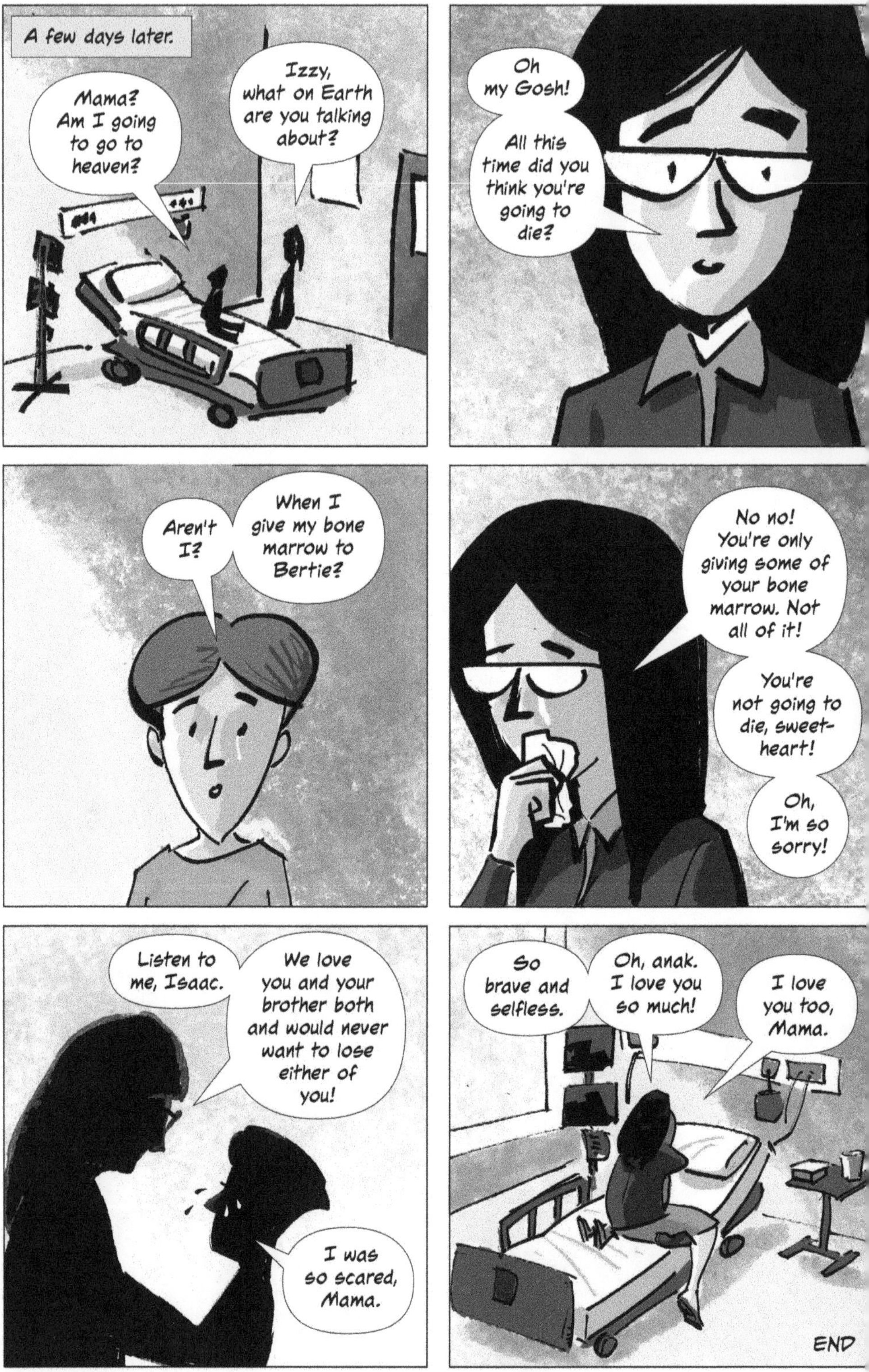
A few days later.
Mama? Am I going to go to heaven?
Izzy, what on Earth are you talking about?
Oh my Gosh!
All this time did you think you're going to die?
Aren't I?
When I give my bone marrow to Bertie?
No no! You're only giving some of your bone marrow. Not all of it!
You're not going to die, sweet-heart!
Oh, I'm so sorry!
Listen to me, Isaac.
We love you and your brother both and would never want to lose either of you!
I was so scared, Mama.
So brave and selfless.
Oh, anak. I love you so much!
I love you too, Mama.
END

Science Check

Bone Marrow Transplants

Also known as Stem Cell Transplants, this is a type of surgery that takes healthy stem cells from one person and gives them to another person who's stem cells aren't able to form new blood cells. Stem cells are important because they can grow into other types of cells. This procedure can be used to replace bone marrow damaged by chemotherapy, radiation or other diseases like lukemia and autoimmune deficiency. It can also kill cancer cells and fight against many cancerous and noncancerous diseases.

The first successful bone marrow transplant was performed by Dr. E. Donnall Thomas in 1958 in Cooperstown, NY. The procedure is harmless to the donor and can be life-saving.

For more information:
http://www.whizkidsdarpa.com/bonemarrow

Chapter Three:
Great Balls of Fire

The group decides to take a break in nature
but accidentally causes a near-catastrophe
if not for some quick thinking and musical talent.

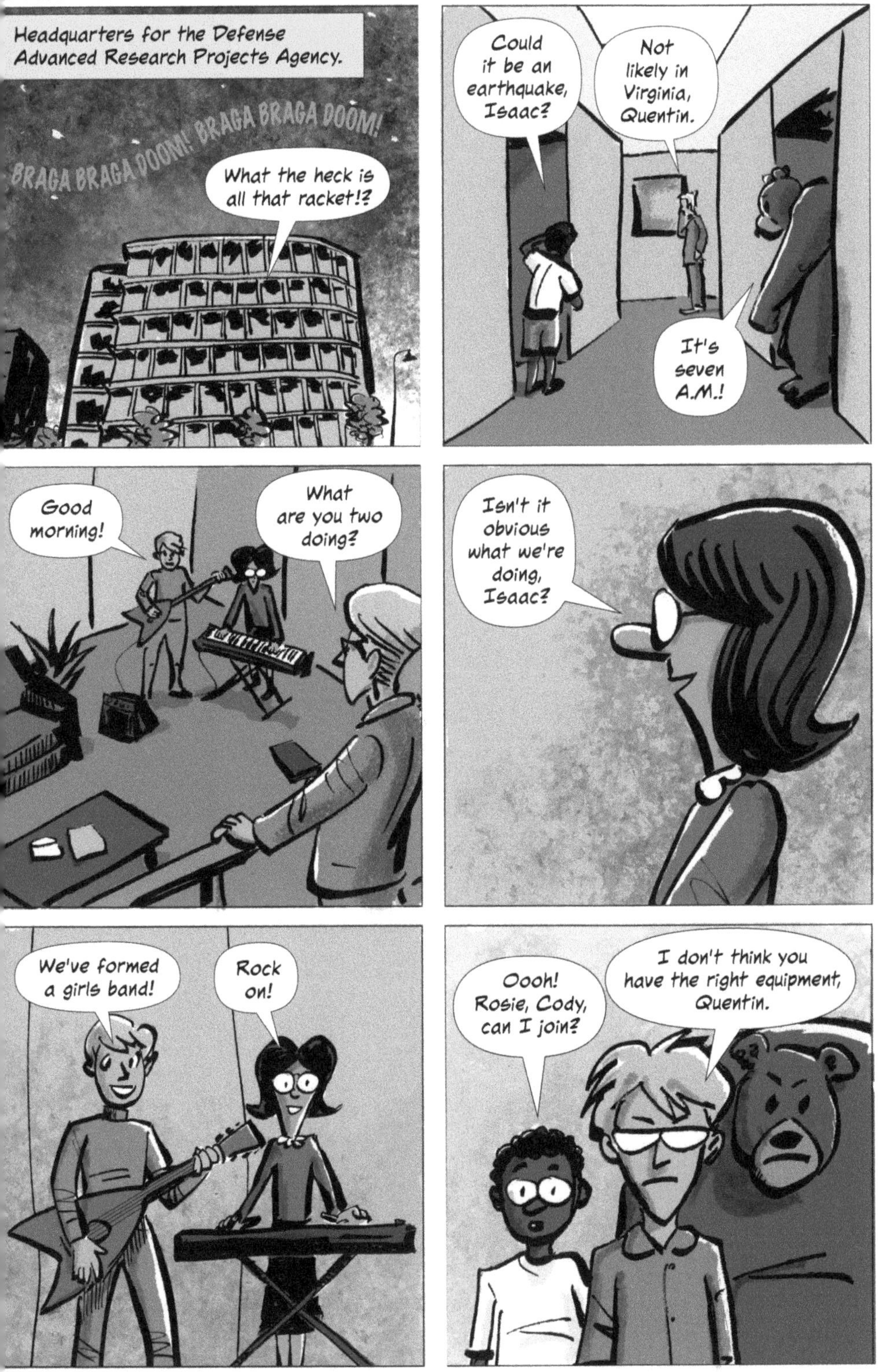
Headquarters for the Defense Advanced Research Projects Agency.
BRAGA BRAGA DOOM! BRAGA BRAGA DOOM!
What the heck is all that racket!?
Could it be an earthquake, Isaac?
Not likely in Virginia, Quentin.
It's seven A.M.!
Good morning!
What are you two doing?
Isn't it obvious what we're doing, Isaac?
We've formed a girls band!
Rock on!
Oooh! Rosie, Cody, can I join?
I don't think you have the right equipment, Quentin.

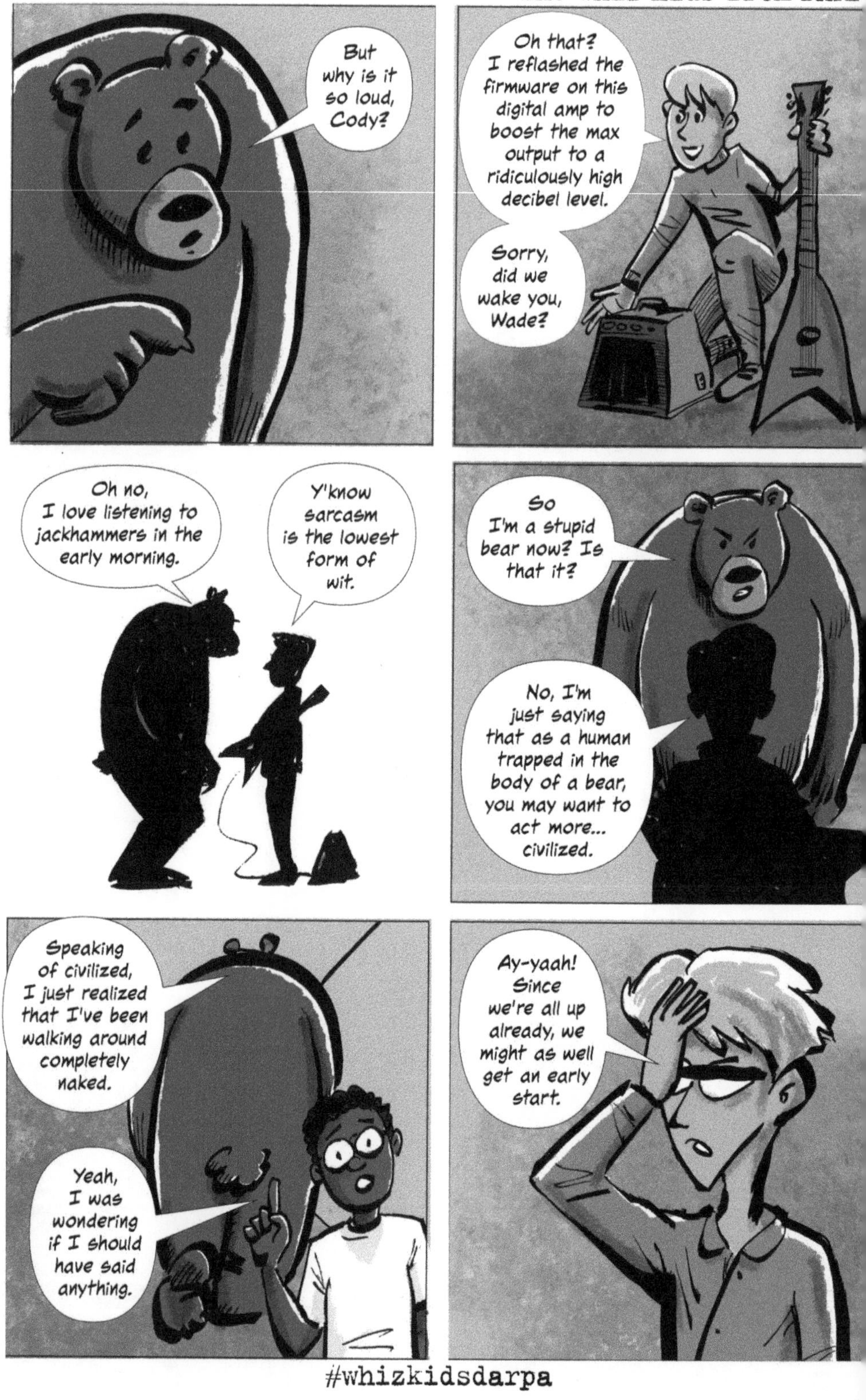
But why is it so loud, Cody?
Oh that? I reflashed the firmware on this digital amp to boost the max output to a ridiculously high decibel level.
Sorry, did we wake you, Wade?
Oh no, I love listening to jackhammers in the early morning.
Y'know sarcasm is the lowest form of wit.
So I'm a stupid bear now? Is that it?
No, I'm just saying that as a human trapped in the body of a bear, you may want to act more... civilized.
Speaking of civilized, I just realized that I've been walking around completely naked.
Yeah, I was wondering if I should have said anything.
Ay-yaah! Since we're all up already, we might as well get an early start.

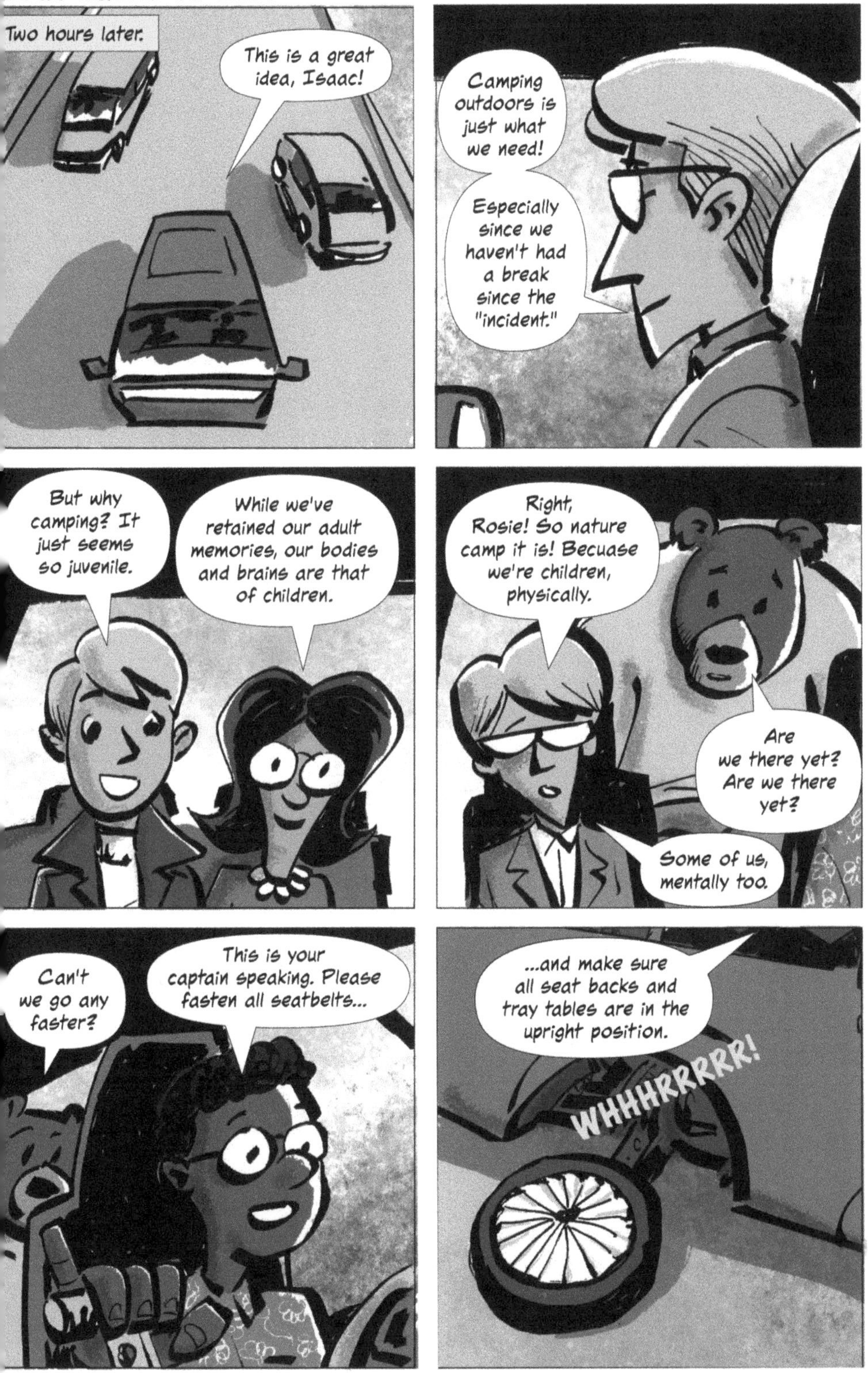
Two hours later.
This is a great idea, Isaac!
Camping outdoors is just what we need!
Especially since we haven't had a break since the "incident."
But why camping? It just seems so juvenile.
While we've retained our adult memories, our bodies and brains are that of children.
Right, Rosie! So nature camp it is! Becuase we're children, physically.
Are we there yet? Are we there yet?
Some of us, mentally too.
Can't we go any faster?
This is your captain speaking. Please fasten all seatbelts...
...and make sure all seat backs and tray tables are in the upright position.
WHHHRRRRR!

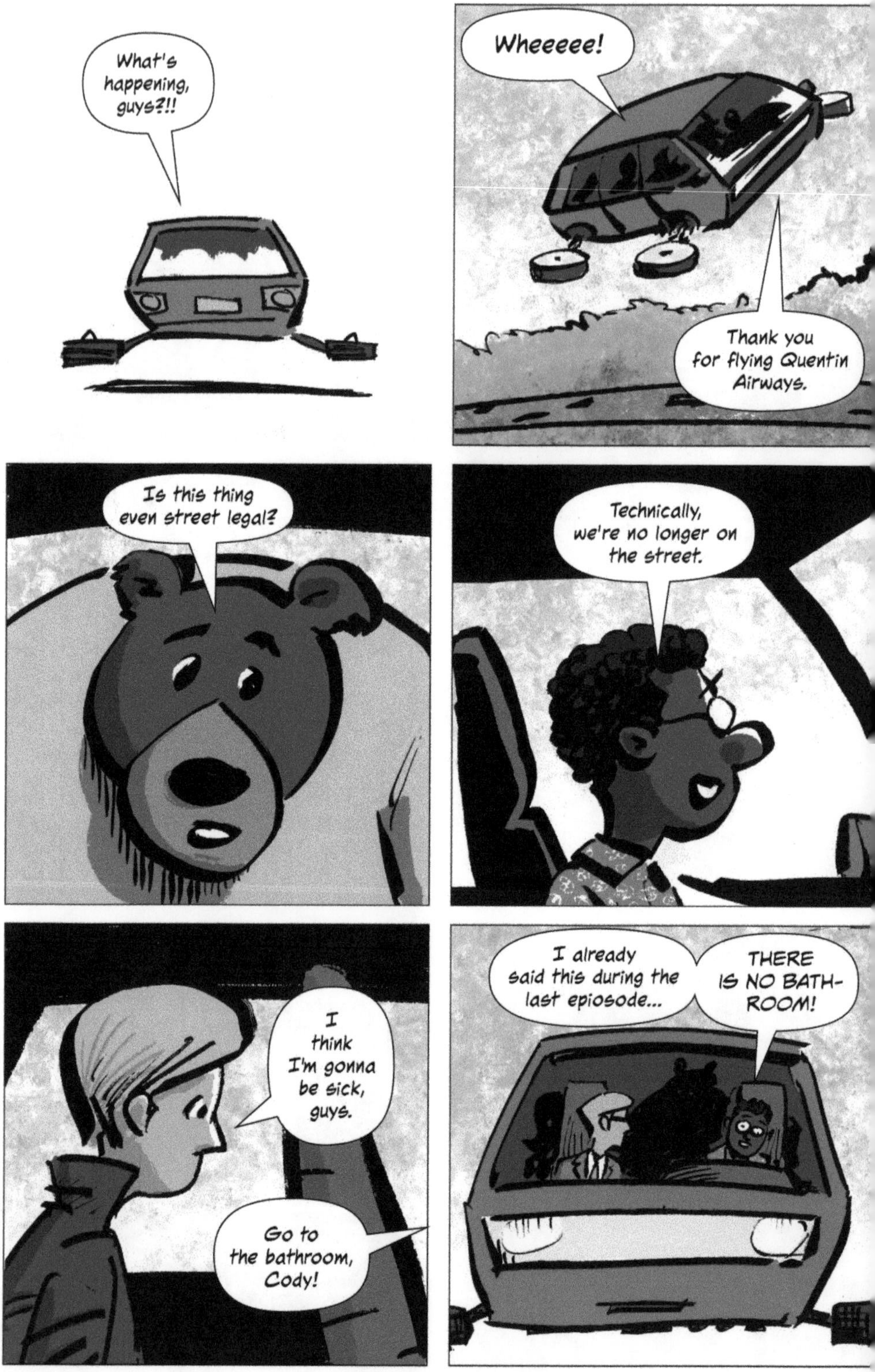
What's happening, guys?!!
Wheeeee!
Thank you for flying Quentin Airways.
Is this thing even street legal?
Technically, we're no longer on the street.
I think I'm gonna be sick, guys.
Go to the bathroom, Cody!
I already said this during the last epiosode...
THERE IS NO BATH-ROOM!

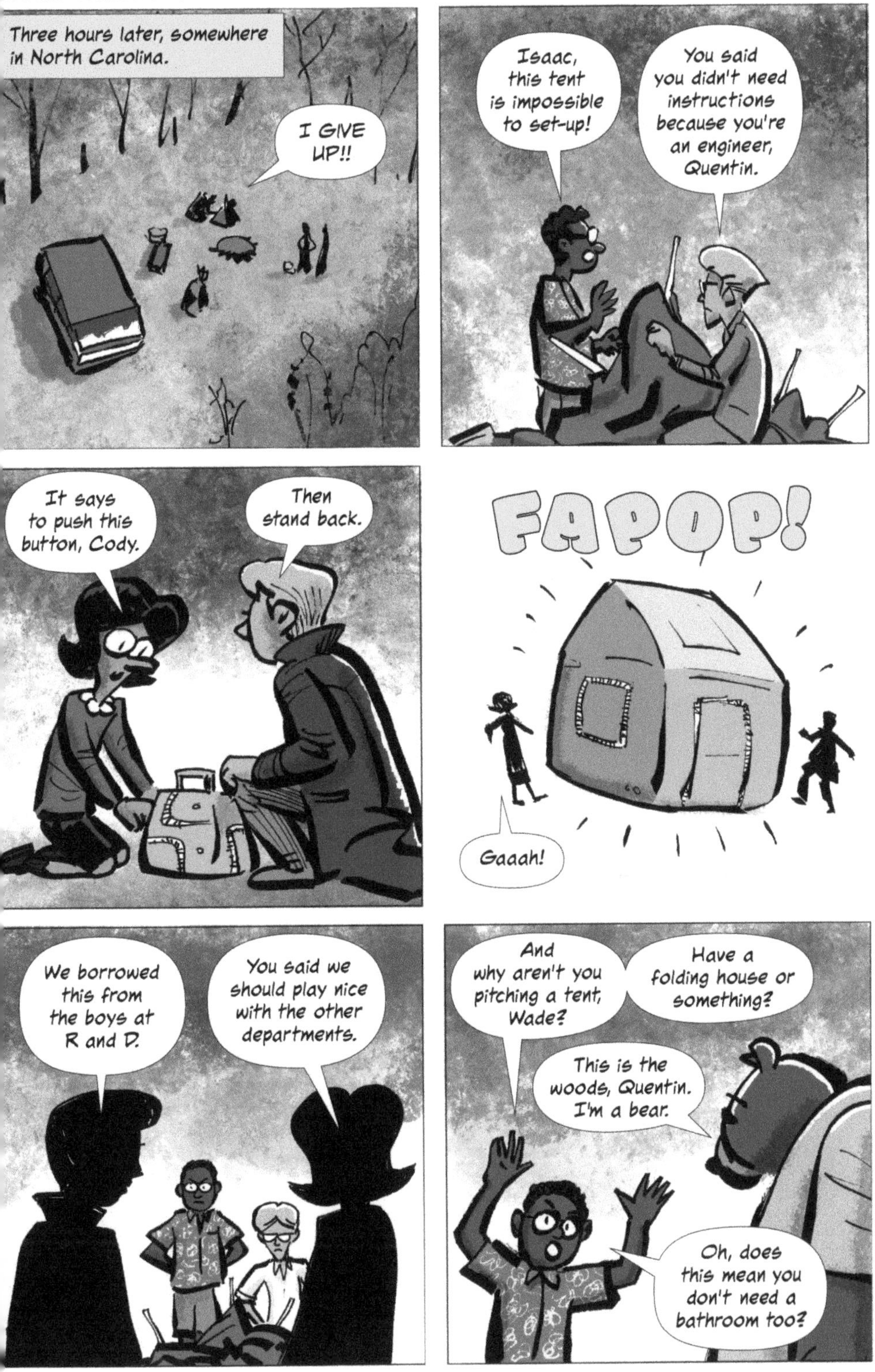
Three hours later, somewhere in North Carolina.
I GIVE UP!!
Isaac, this tent is impossible to set-up!
You said you didn't need instructions because you're an engineer, Quentin.
It says to push this button, Cody.
Then stand back.
FAPOP!
Gaaah!
We borrowed this from the boys at R and D.
You said we should play nice with the other departments.
And why aren't you pitching a tent, Wade?
Have a folding house or something?
This is the woods, Quentin. I'm a bear.
Oh, does this mean you don't need a bathroom too?

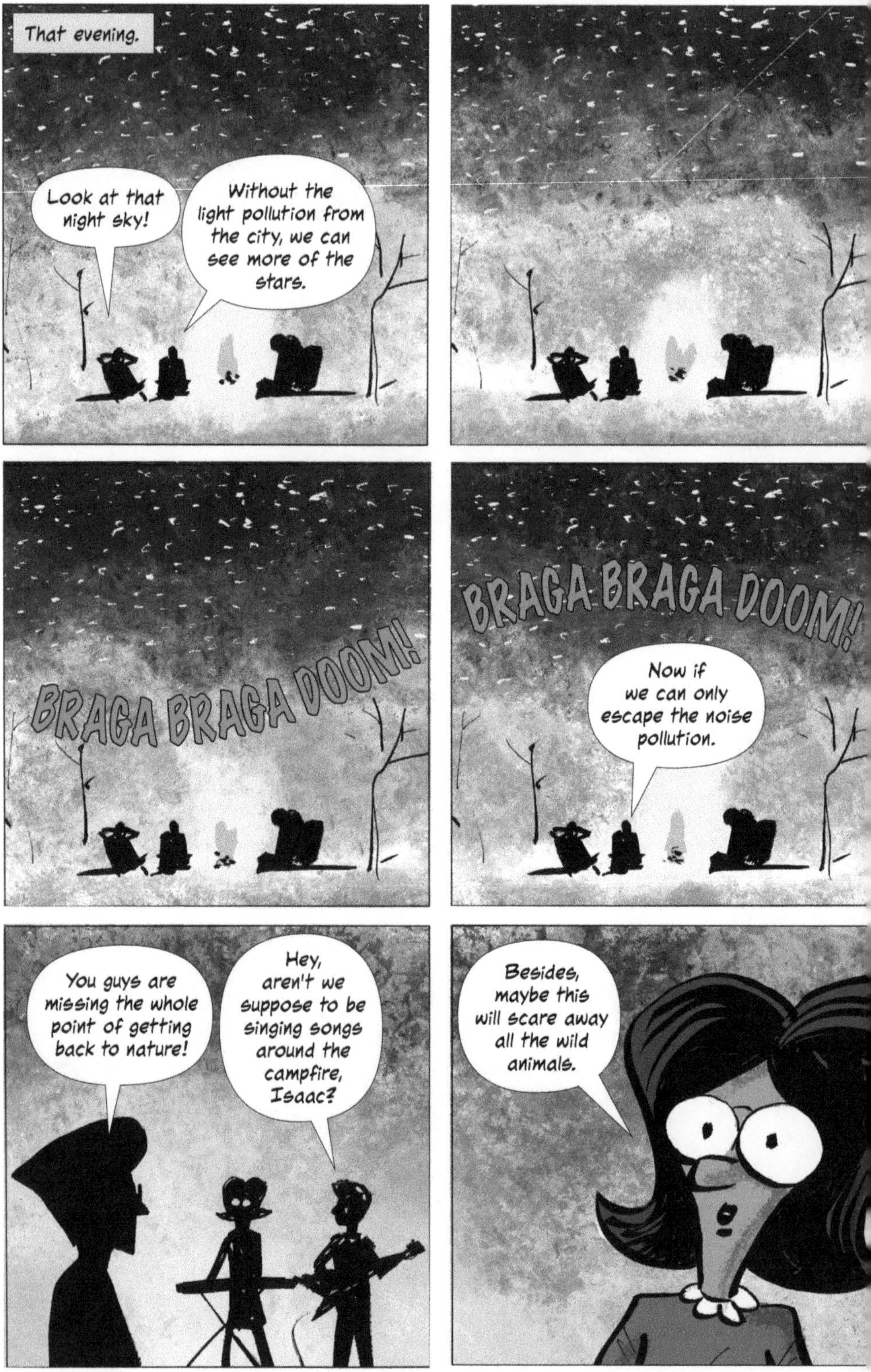
That evening.
Look at that night sky!
Without the light pollution from the city, we can see more of the stars.
BRAGA BRAGA DOOM!
BRAGA BRAGA DOOM!
Now if we can only escape the noise pollution.
You guys are missing the whole point of getting back to nature!
Hey, aren't we suppose to be singing songs around the campfire, Isaac?
Besides, maybe this will scare away all the wild animals.

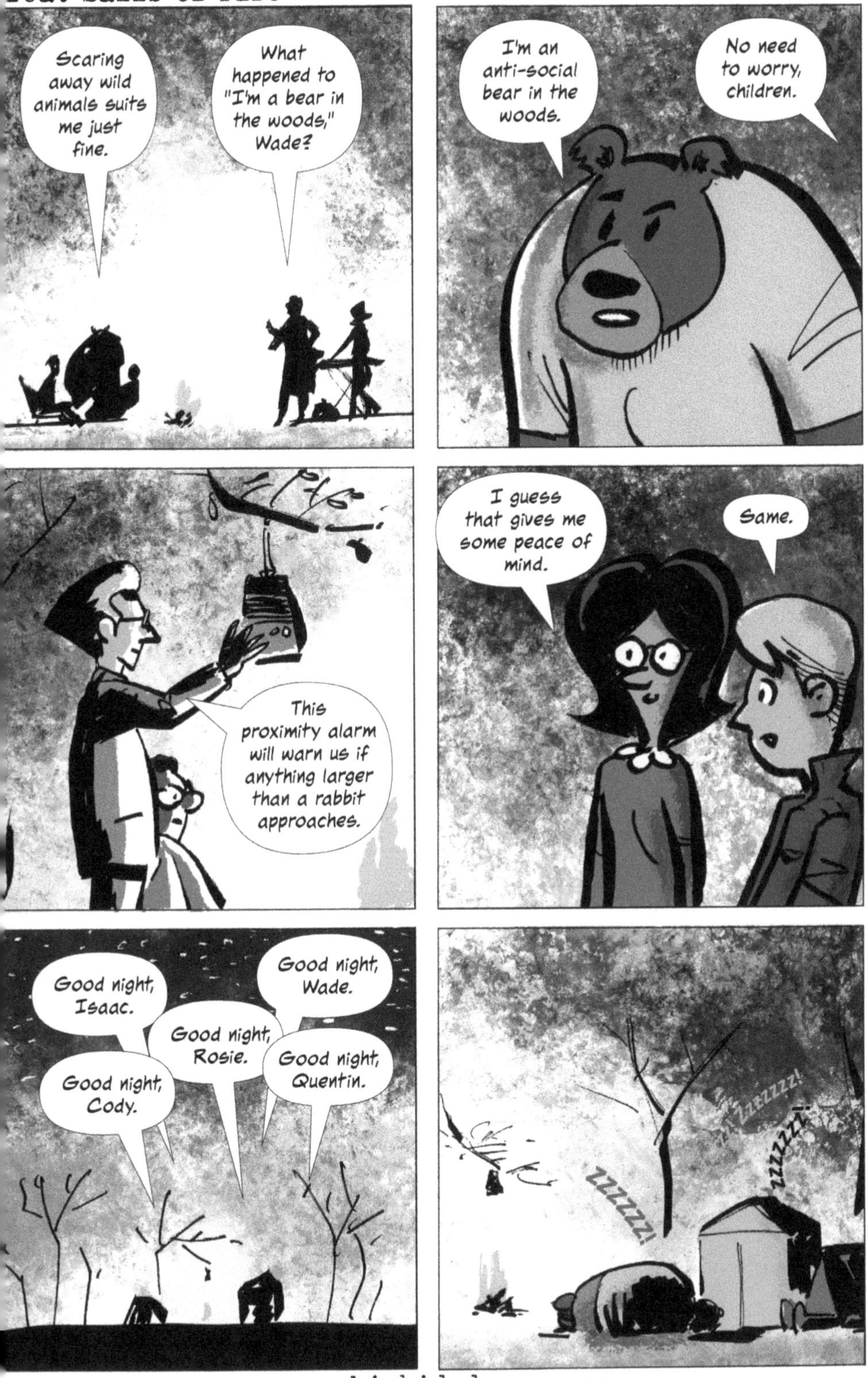
Scaring away wild animals suits me just fine.
What happened to "I'm a bear in the woods," Wade?
I'm an anti-social bear in the woods.
No need to worry, children.
This proximity alarm will warn us if anything larger than a rabbit approaches.
I guess that gives me some peace of mind.
Same.
Good night, Isaac.
Good night, Wade.
Good night, Rosie.
Good night, Cody.
Good night, Quentin.
ZZZZZZ!
ZZZZZZZ!
ZZZZZZZ

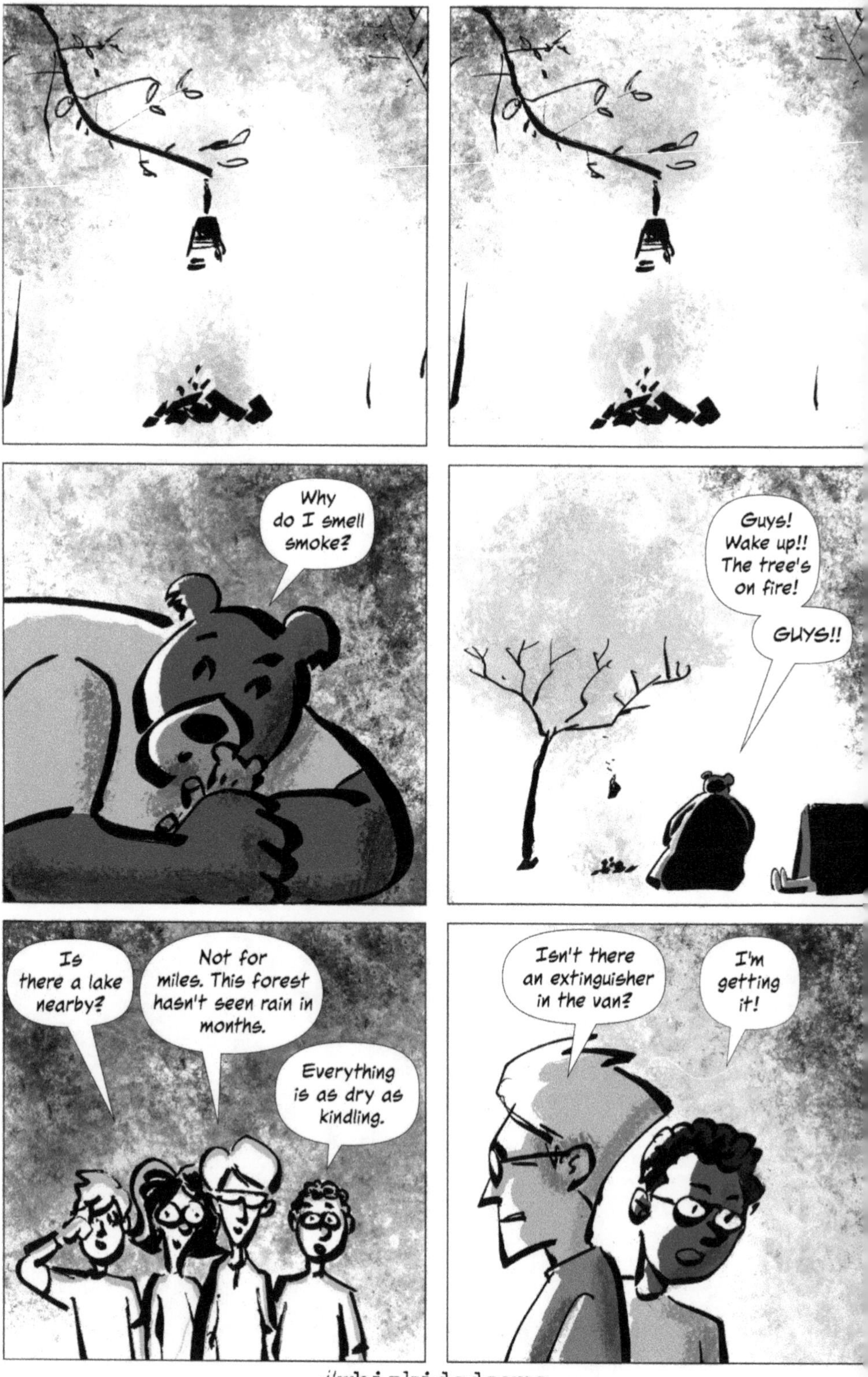
Why do I smell smoke?
Guys! Wake up!! The tree's on fire!
GUYS!!
Is there a lake nearby?
Not for miles. This forest hasn't seen rain in months.
Everything is as dry as kindling.
Isn't there an extinguisher in the van?
I'm getting it!

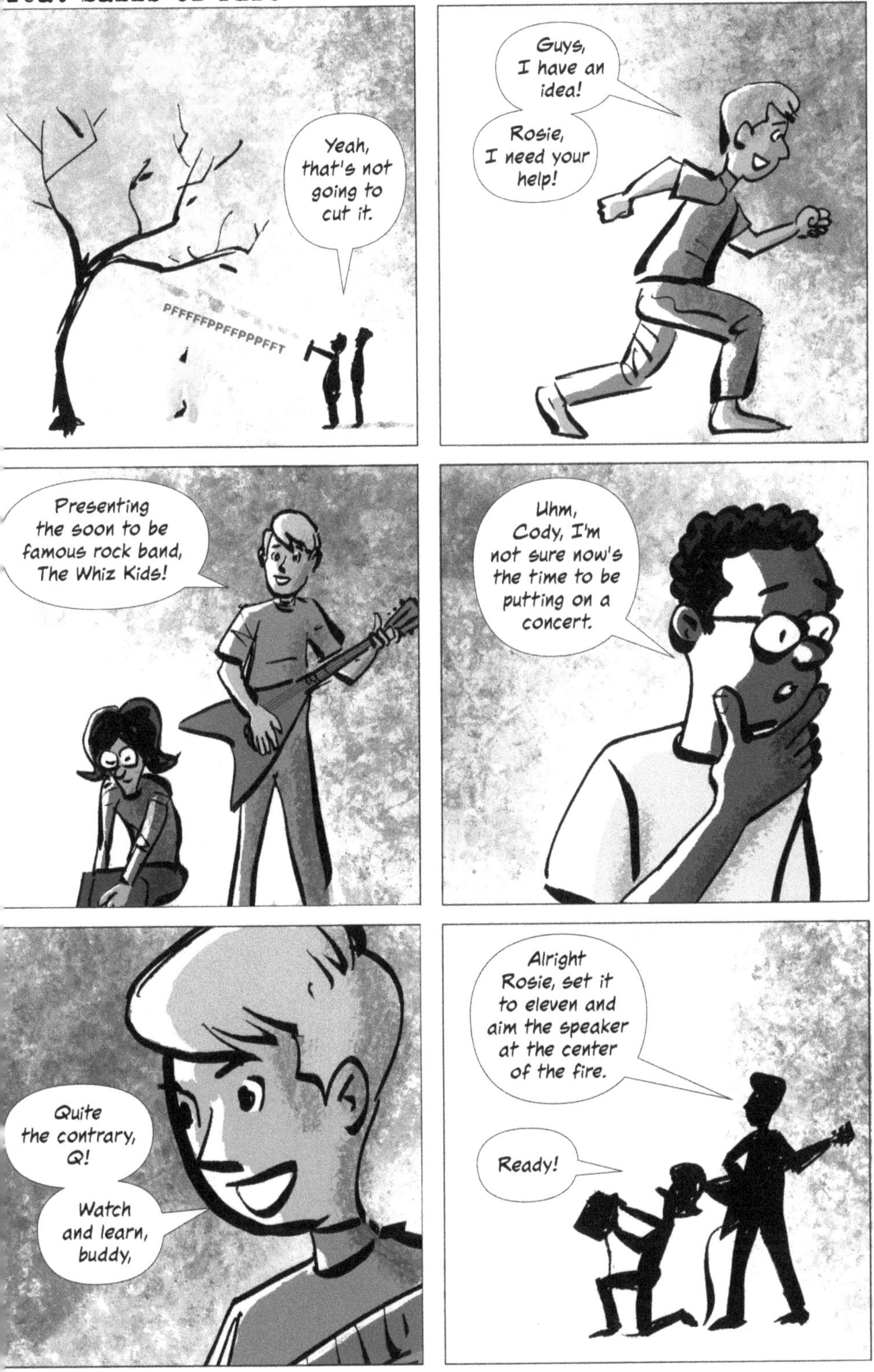
Yeah, that's not going to cut it.
PFFFFFPPFFPPPFFT
Guys, I have an idea!
Rosie, I need your help!
Presenting the soon to be famous rock band, The Whiz Kids!
Uhm, Cody, I'm not sure now's the time to be putting on a concert.
Quite the contrary, Q!
Watch and learn, buddy,
Alright Rosie, set it to eleven and aim the speaker at the center of the fire.
Ready!

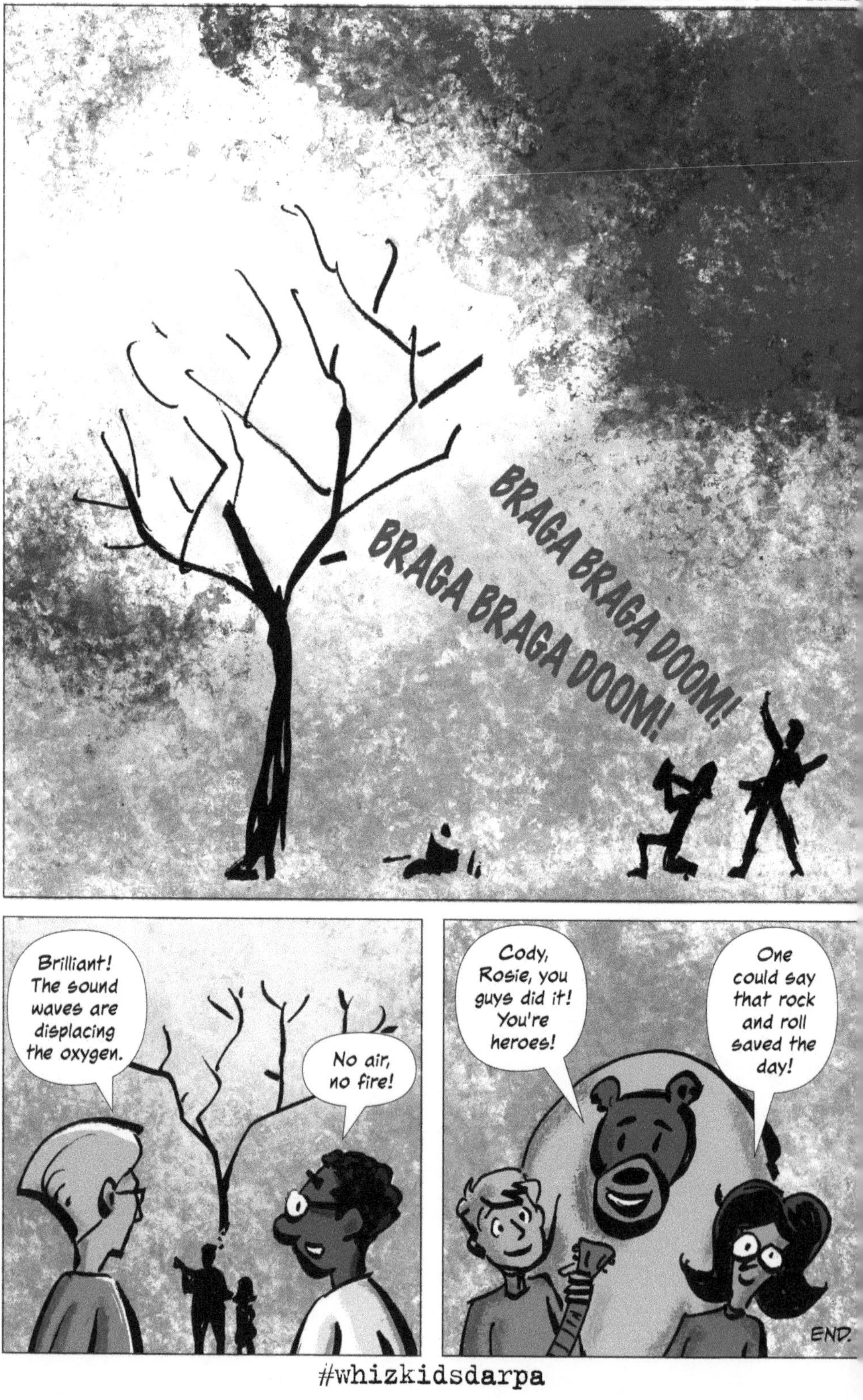
BRAGA BRAGA DOOM!
BRAGA BRAGA DOOM!
Brilliant! The sound waves are displacing the oxygen.
No air, no fire!
Cody, Rosie, you guys did it! You're heroes!
One could say that rock and roll saved the day!
END.

#whizkidsdarpa

Science Check

Using Soundwaves Against Fires

Sound produces vibrations through matter like solids and air. These vibrations are physical and can move and push things like oxygen which is needed by fire. By using sound to push oxygen away, you can extinguish a fire. This method is ideal because it requires no water or chemicals and does virtually no damage to property.

While there have been previous attempts at making acoustic fire extinguishers, a successful version was finally made by two George Mason University engineering students, Viet Tran & Seth Robertson, in 2015. Originally made to stop house fires, it soon evolved to be utilized in fighting forest fires. Unlike previous tries, these working acoustic fire extinguishers use low frequency sounds.

For more information:
http://www.whizkidsdarpa.com/soundwaves

Chapter Four:

Cody

Cody uses this second chance at childhood
and decides to live their life truer to what they feel.

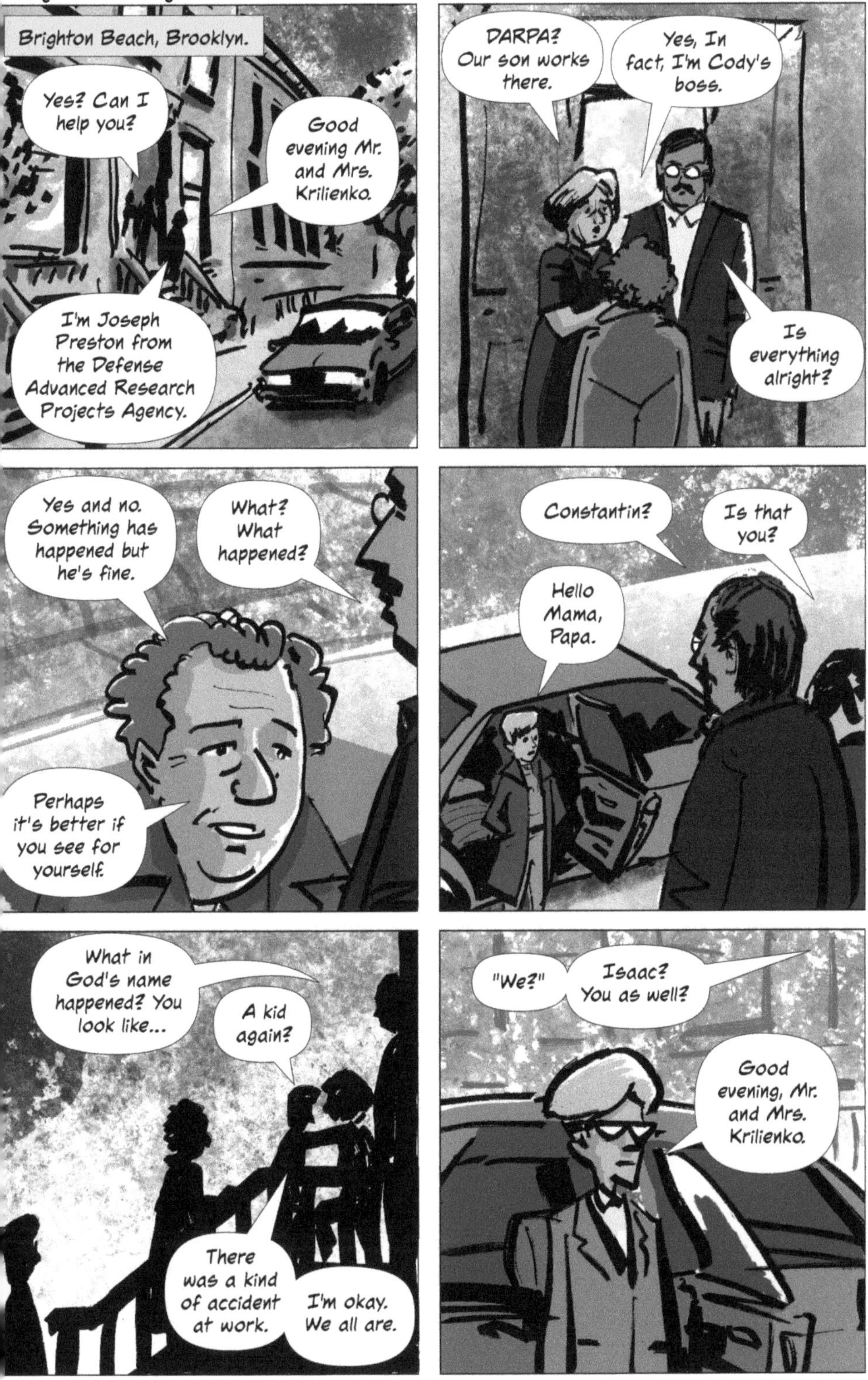
Brighton Beach, Brooklyn.
Yes? Can I help you?
Good evening Mr. and Mrs. Krilienko.
I'm Joseph Preston from the Defense Advanced Research Projects Agency.
DARPA? Our son works there.
Yes, In fact, I'm Cody's boss.
Is everything alright?
Yes and no. Something has happened but he's fine.
What? What happened?
Perhaps it's better if you see for yourself.
Constantin?
Is that you?
Hello Mama, Papa.
What in God's name happened? You look like...
A kid again?
There was a kind of accident at work.
I'm okay. We all are.
"We?"
Isaac? You as well?
Good evening, Mr. and Mrs. Krilienko.

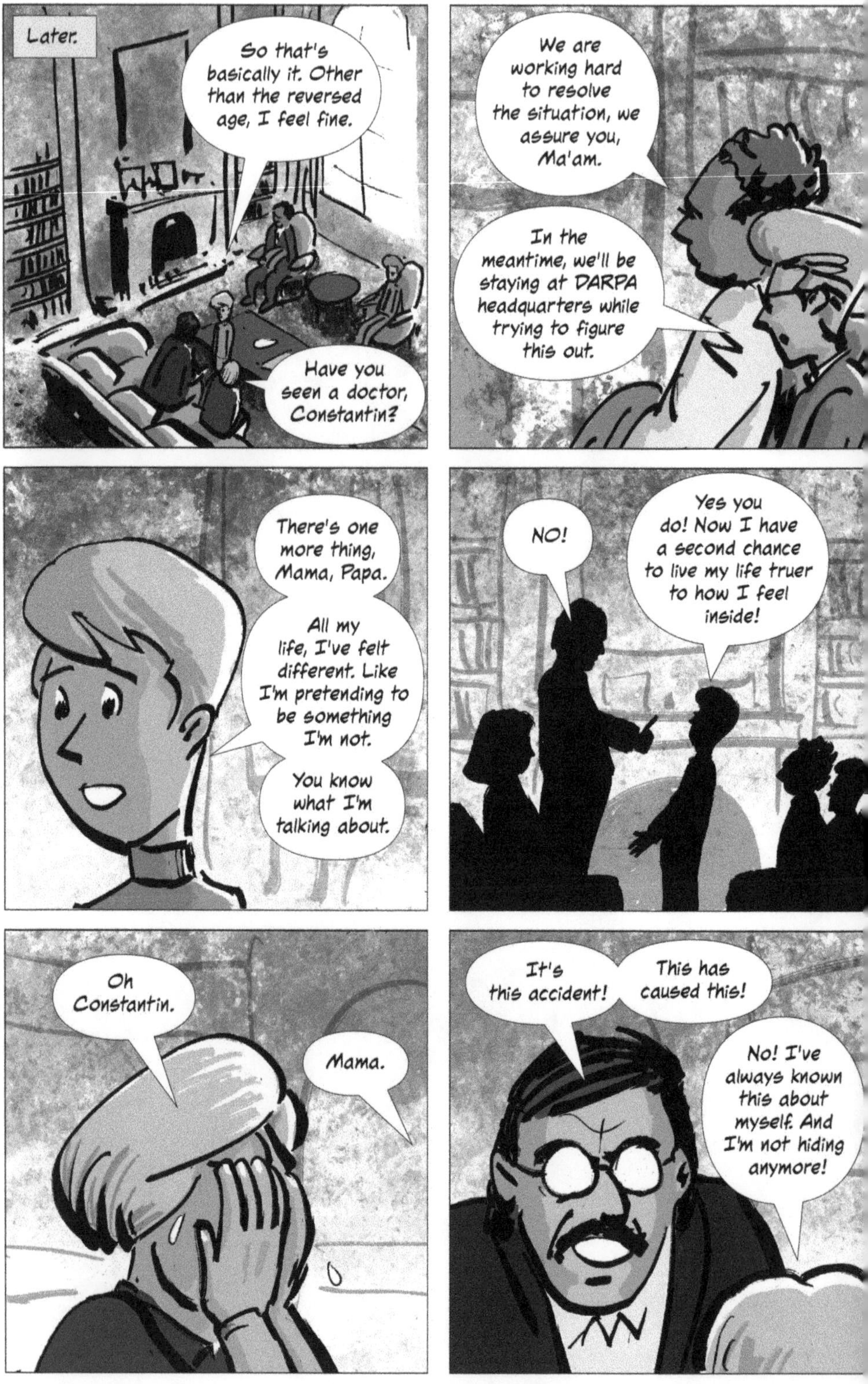
Later.
So that's basically it. Other than the reversed age, I feel fine.
Have you seen a doctor, Constantin?
We are working hard to resolve the situation, we assure you, Ma'am.
In the meantime, we'll be staying at DARPA headquarters while trying to figure this out.
There's one more thing, Mama, Papa.
All my life, I've felt different. Like I'm pretending to be something I'm not.
You know what I'm talking about.
NO!
Yes you do! Now I have a second chance to live my life truer to how I feel inside!
Oh Constantin.
Mama.
It's this accident!
This has caused this!
No! I've always known this about myself. And I'm not hiding anymore!

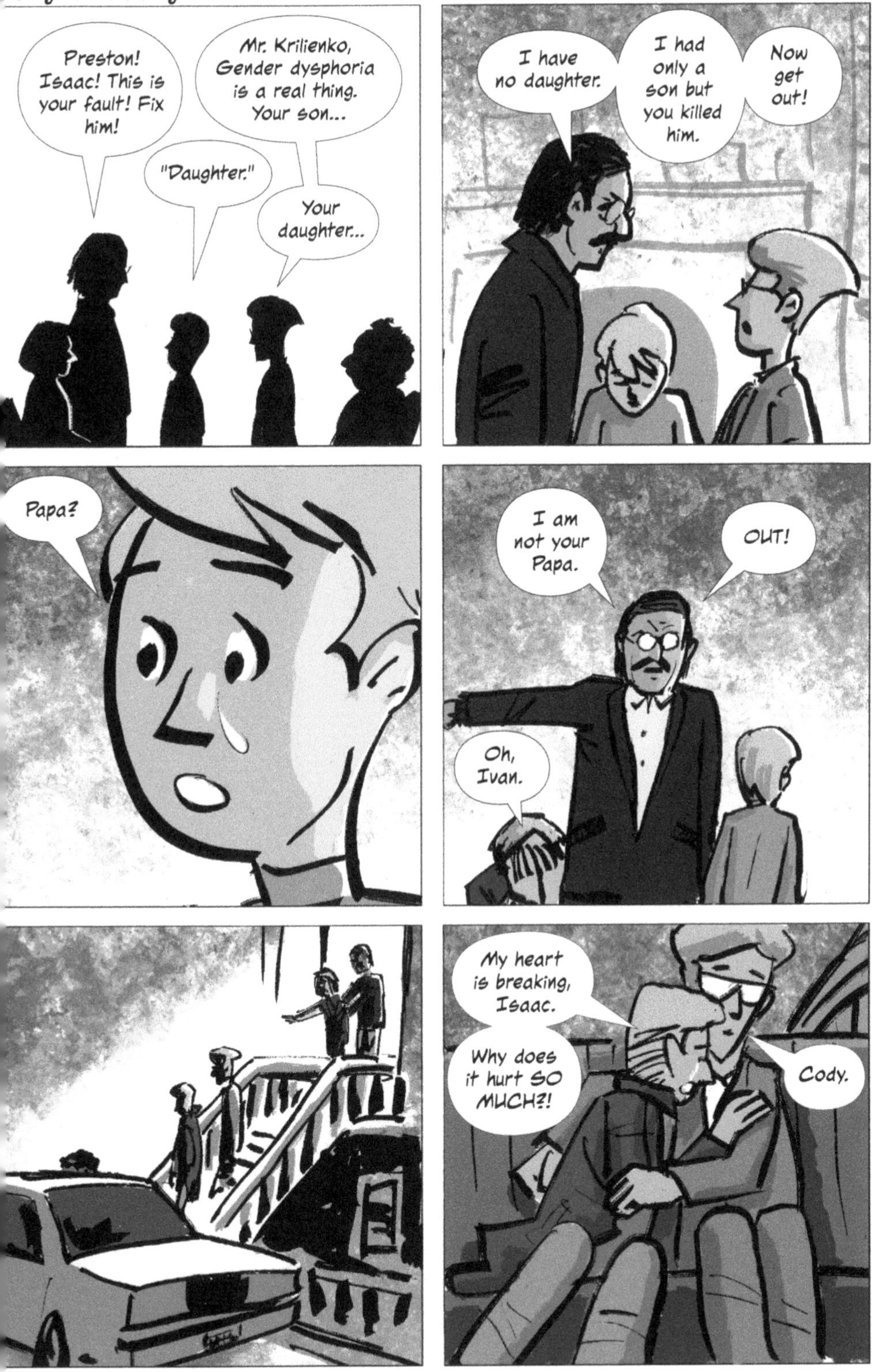
Preston! Isaac! This is your fault! Fix him!
Mr. Krilienko, Gender dysphoria is a real thing. Your son...
"Daughter."
Your daughter...
I have no daughter.
I had only a son but you killed him.
Now get out!
Papa?
I am not your Papa.
OUT!
Oh, Ivan.
My heart is breaking, Isaac.
Why does it hurt SO MUCH?!
Cody.

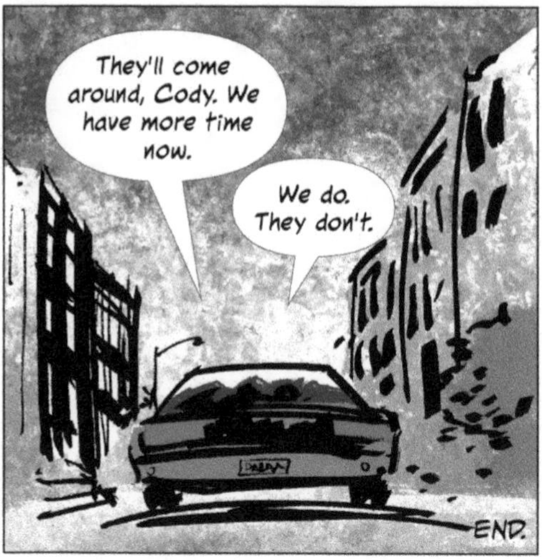
They'll come around, Cody. We have more time now.
We do. They don't.
END.

Science Check

Gender Dysphoria

Gender Dysphoria is when somebody experiences distress and discomfort in their own body due to conflict with their gender assigned at birth and the gender that they feel inside. People with Gender Dysphoria, usually want to match their gender identity with the gender they feel they truly are. This can mean changing their pronoun, their name, their appearance and/or their lifestyle.

While not considered a mental illness, Gender Dysphoria can cause the development of other issues such as emotional distress, anxiety and depression.

For more information:
http://www.whizkidsdarpa.com/dysphoria

Chapter Five:
First Contact

Our young intrepid scientists are sent to investigate sightings
of extra-terrestrials and try to make contact with them.

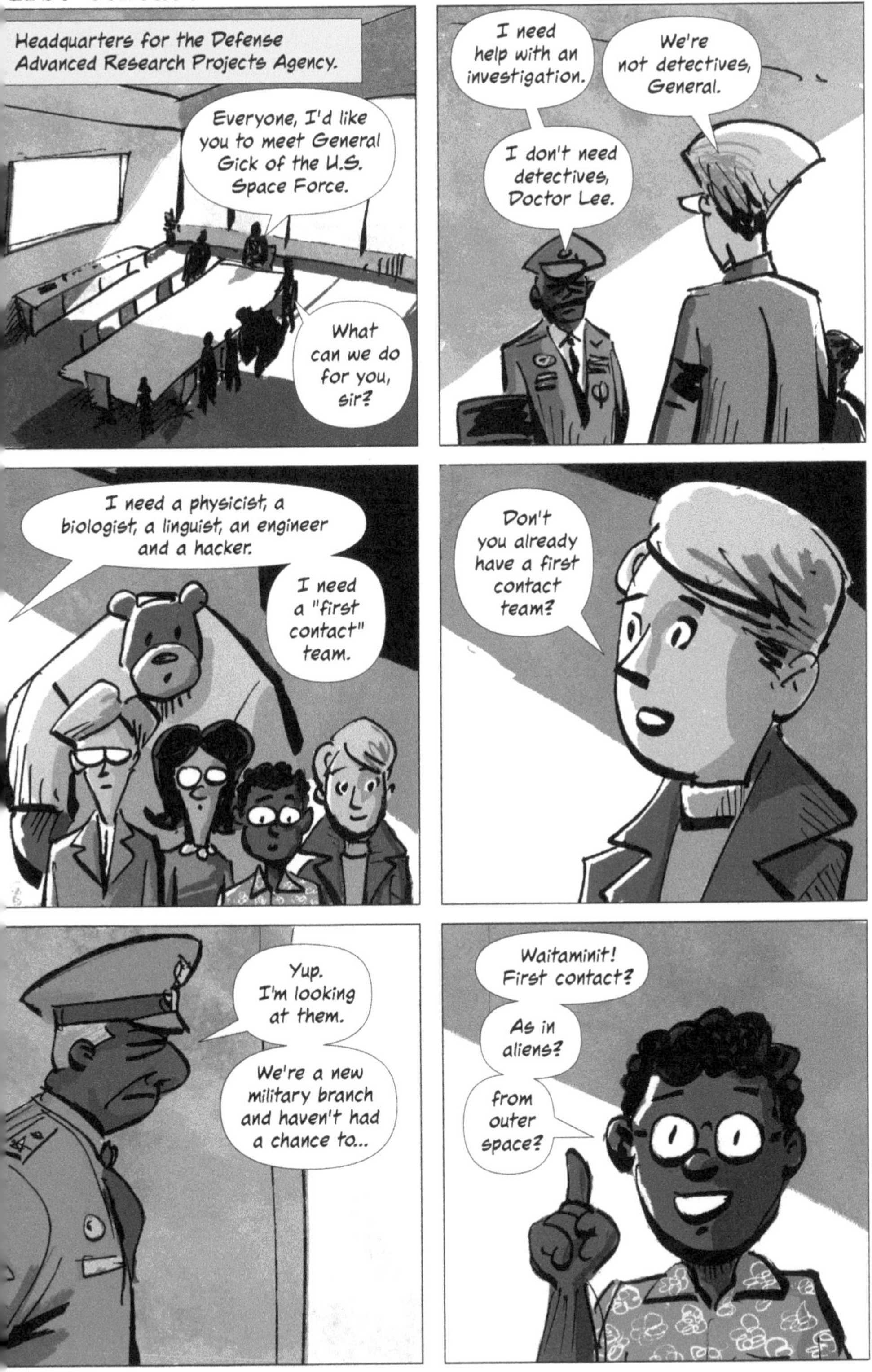
Headquarters for the Defense Advanced Research Projects Agency.
Everyone, I'd like you to meet General Gick of the U.S. Space Force.
What can we do for you, sir?
I need help with an investigation.
We're not detectives, General.
I don't need detectives, Doctor Lee.
I need a physicist, a biologist, a linguist, an engineer and a hacker.
I need a "first contact" team.
Don't you already have a first contact team?
Yup. I'm looking at them.
We're a new military branch and haven't had a chance to...
Waitaminit! First contact?
As in aliens?
from outer space?

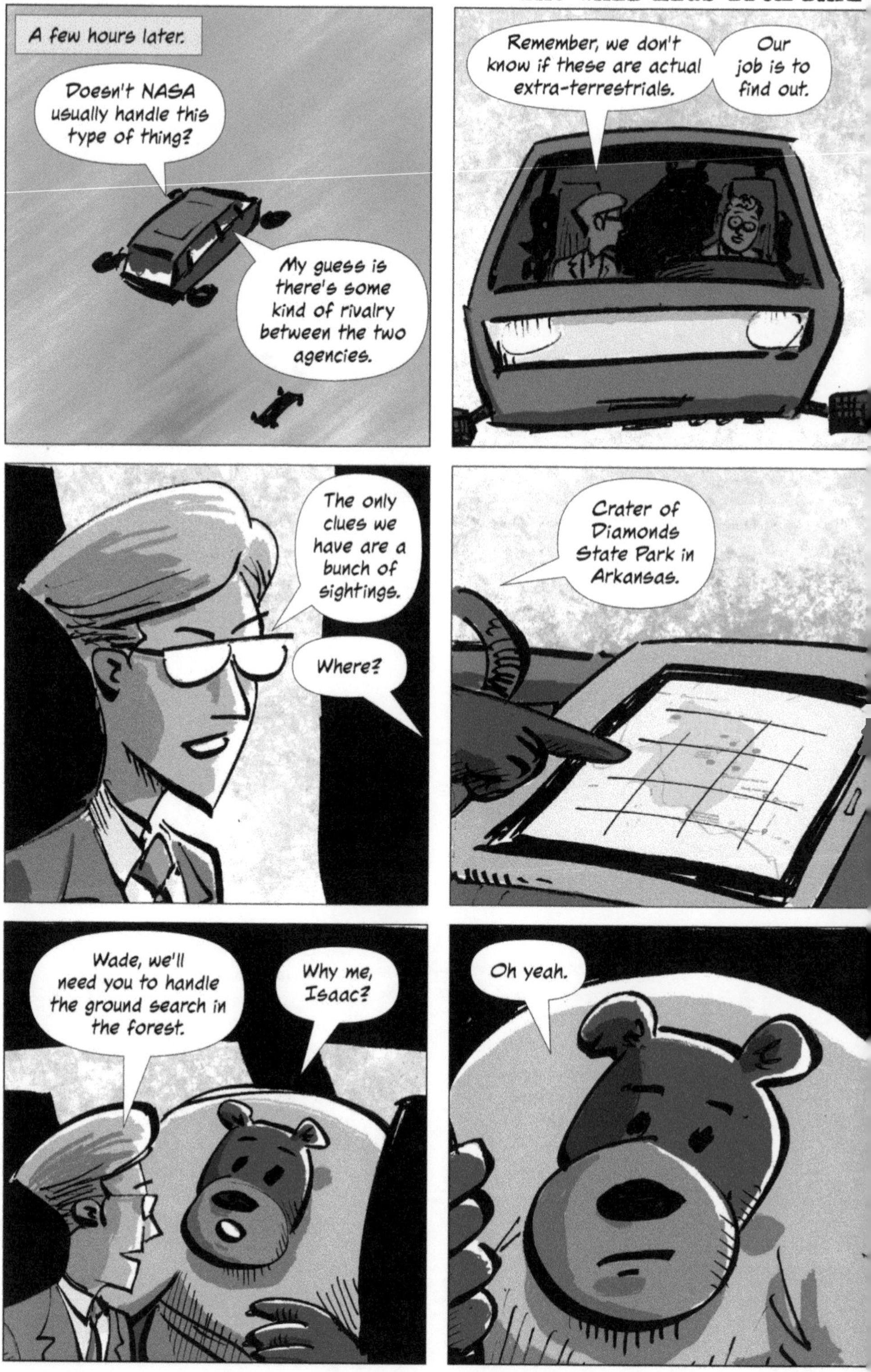
A few hours later.
Doesn't NASA usually handle this type of thing?
My guess is there's some kind of rivalry between the two agencies.
Remember, we don't know if these are actual extra-terrestrials.
Our job is to find out.
The only clues we have are a bunch of sightings.
Where?
Crater of Diamonds State Park in Arkansas.
Wade, we'll need you to handle the ground search in the forest.
Why me, Isaac?
Oh yeah.

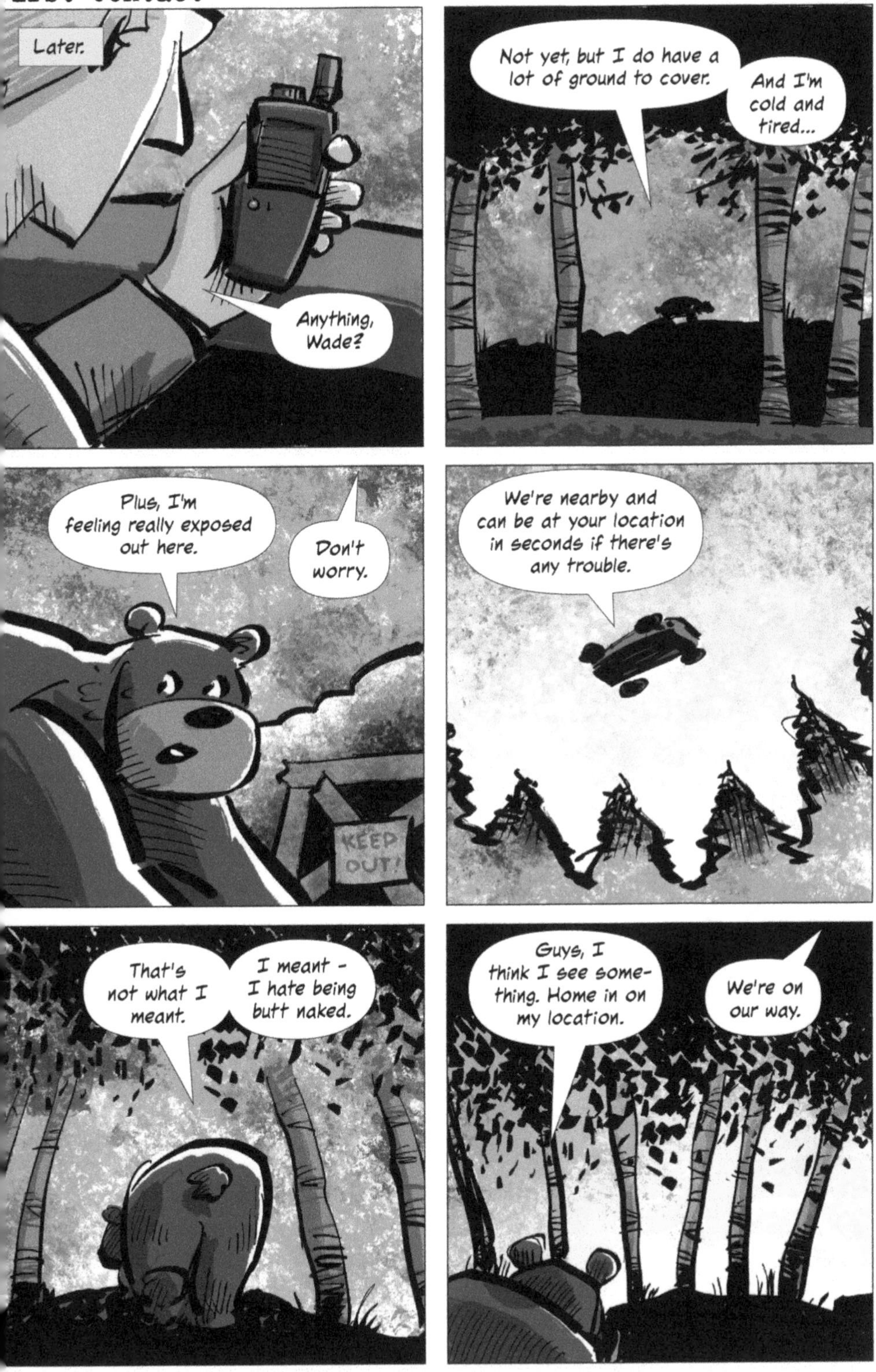
Later.
Anything, Wade?
Not yet, but I do have a lot of ground to cover.
And I'm cold and tired...
Plus, I'm feeling really exposed out here.
Don't worry.
KEEP OUT!
We're nearby and can be at your location in seconds if there's any trouble.
That's not what I meant.
I meant - I hate being butt naked.
Guys, I think I see something. Home in on my location.
We're on our way.

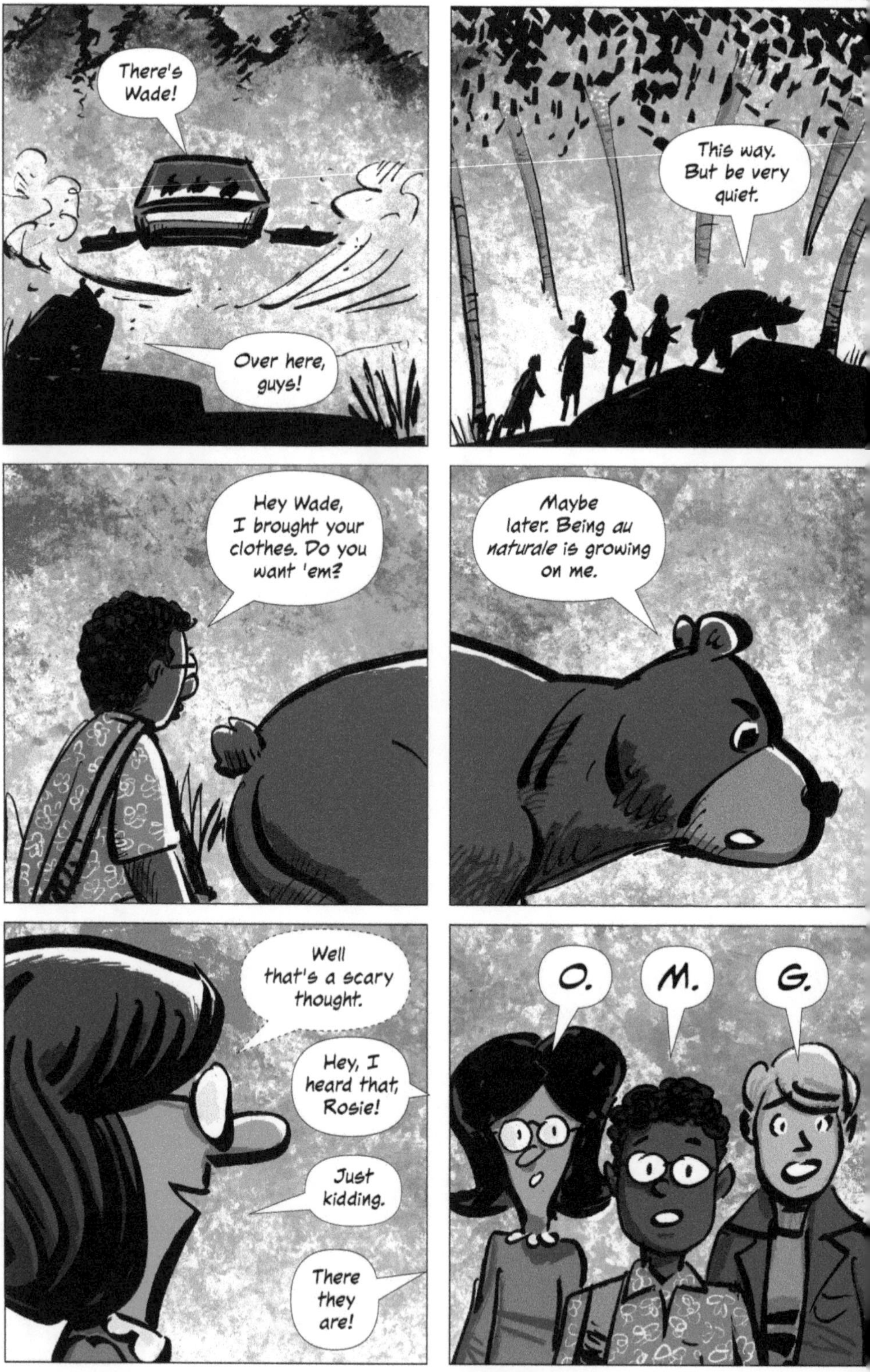
There's Wade!
Over here, guys!
This way. But be very quiet.
Hey Wade, I brought your clothes. Do you want 'em?
Maybe later. Being *au naturale* is growing on me.
Well that's a scary thought.
Hey, I heard that, Rosie!
Just kidding.
There they are!
O.
M.
G.

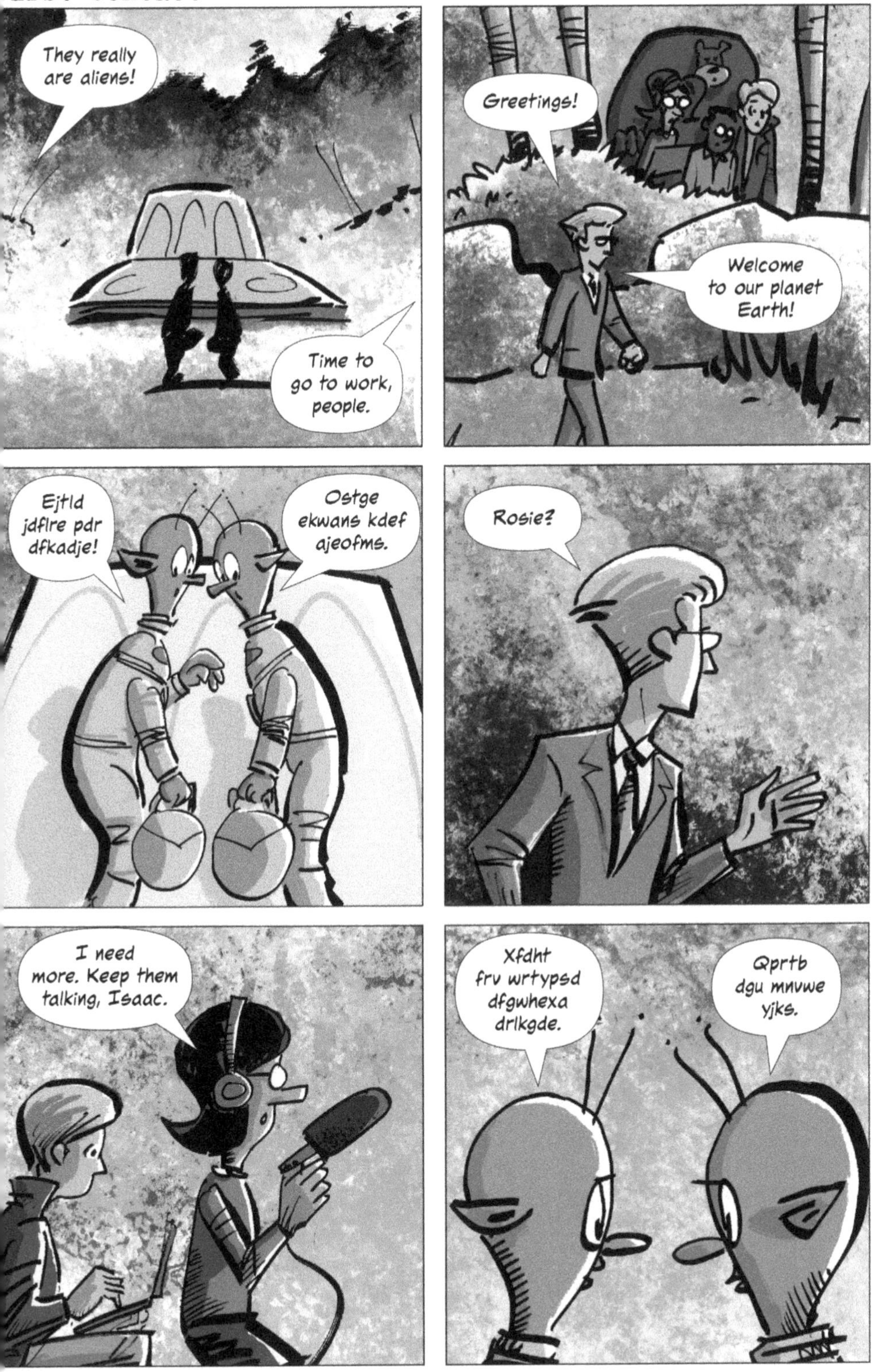
They really are aliens!
Time to go to work, people.
Greetings!
Welcome to our planet Earth!
Ejtld jdflre pdr dfkadje!
Ostge ekwans kdef ajeofms.
Rosie?
I need more. Keep them talking, Isaac.
Xfdht frv wrtypsd dfgwhexa drlkgde.
Qprtb dgu mnvwe yjks.

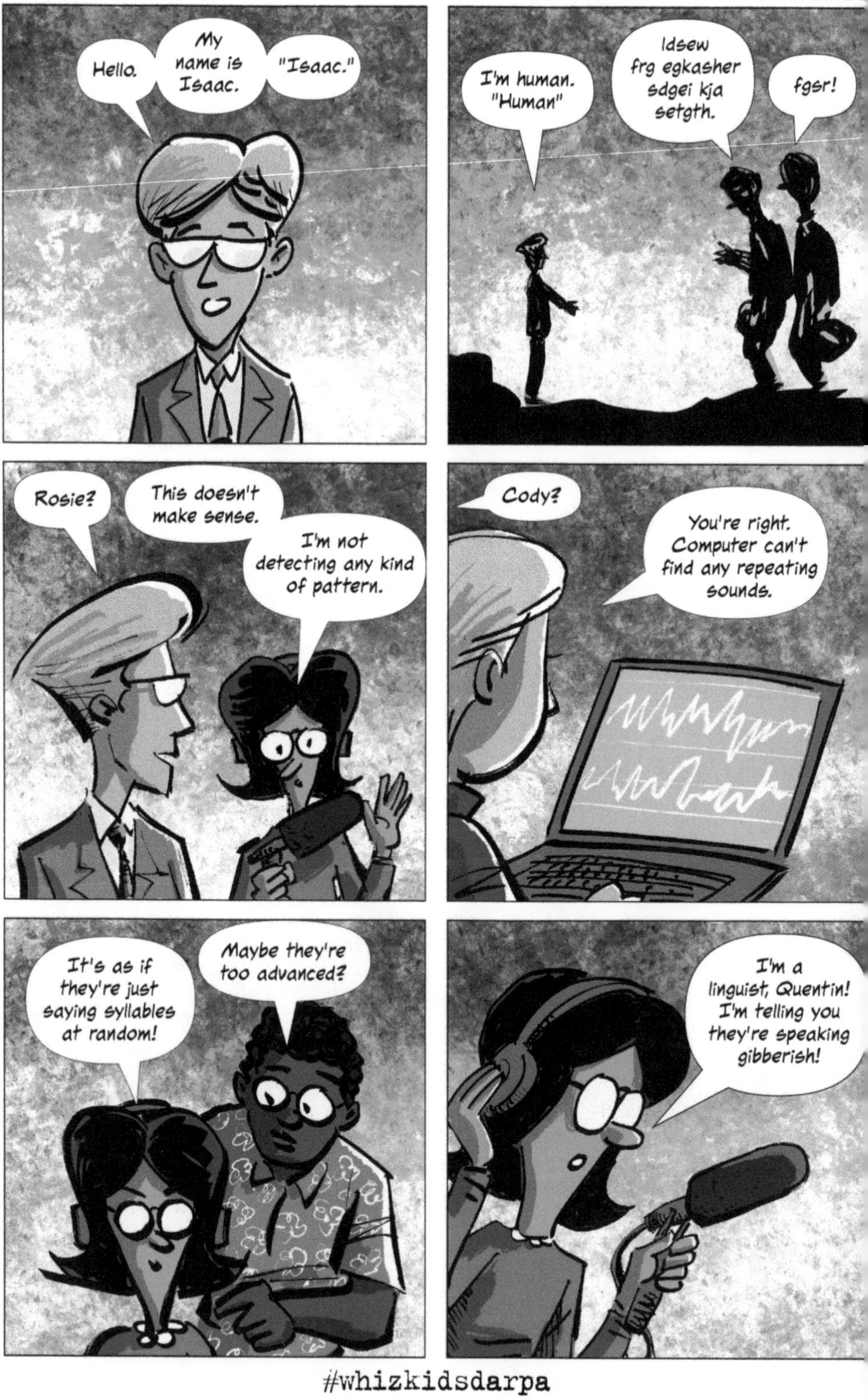
Hello.
My name is Isaac.
"Isaac."
I'm human. "Human"
ldsew frg egkasher sdgei kja setgth.
fgsr!
Rosie?
This doesn't make sense.
I'm not detecting any kind of pattern.
Cody?
You're right. Computer can't find any repeating sounds.
It's as if they're just saying syllables at random!
Maybe they're too advanced?
I'm a linguist, Quentin! I'm telling you they're speaking gibberish!

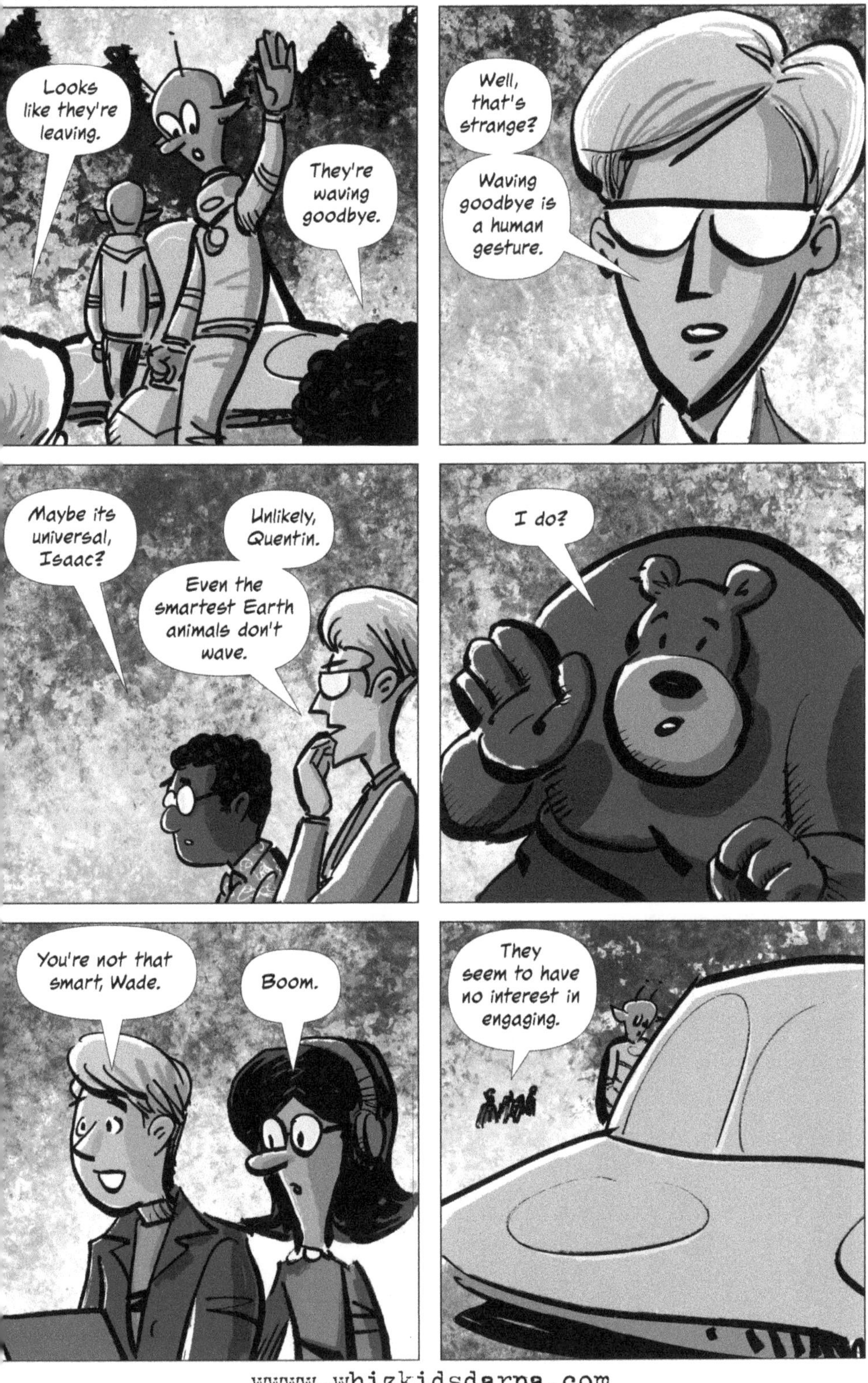
Looks like they're leaving.
They're waving goodbye.
Well, that's strange?
Waving goodbye is a human gesture.
Maybe its universal, Isaac?
Unlikely, Quentin.
Even the smartest Earth animals don't wave.
I do?
You're not that smart, Wade.
Boom.
They seem to have no interest in engaging.

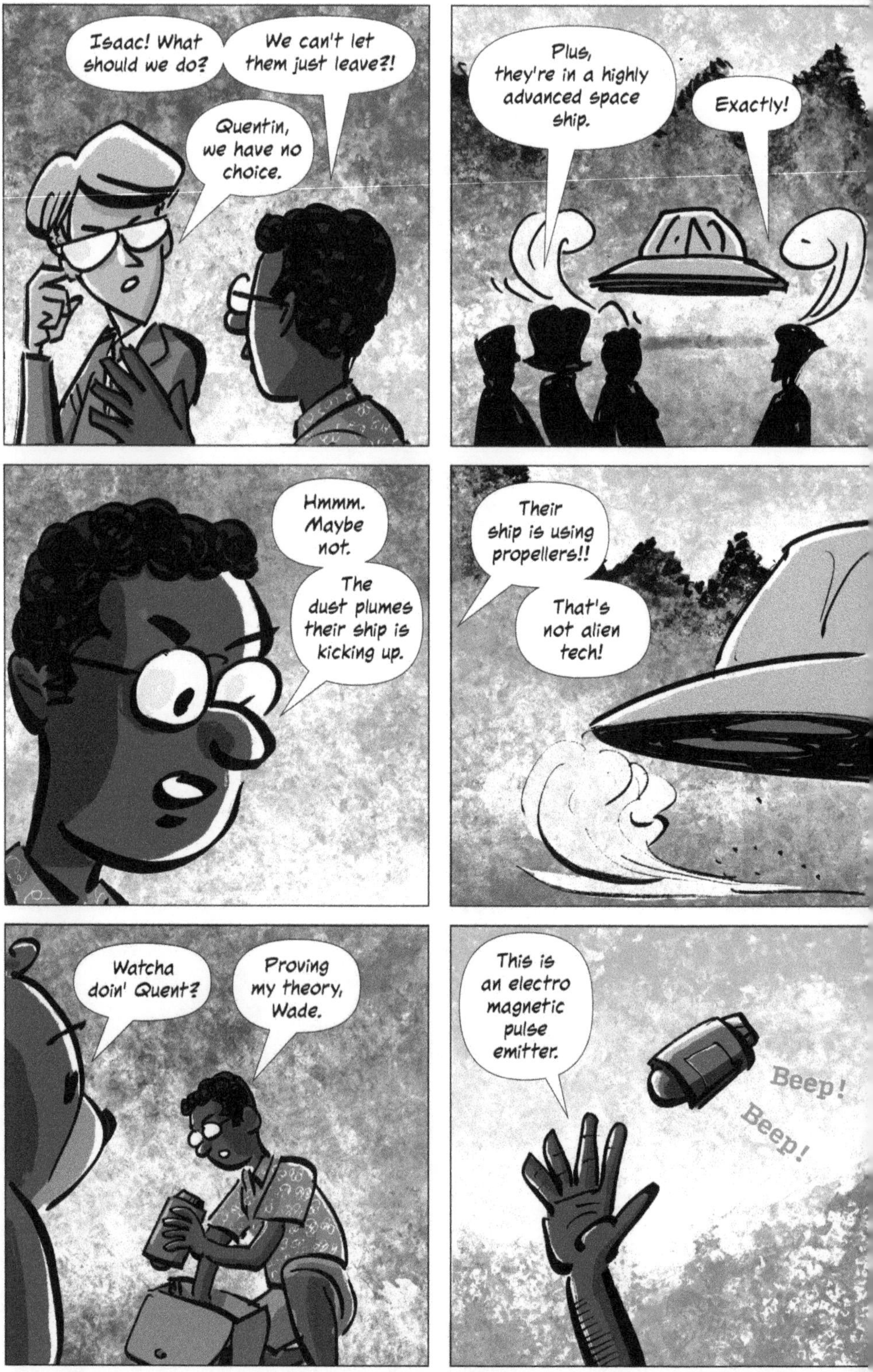
Isaac! What should we do?
We can't let them just leave?!
Quentin, we have no choice.
Plus, they're in a highly advanced space ship.
Exactly!
Hmmm. Maybe not.
The dust plumes their ship is kicking up.
Their ship is using propellers!!
That's not alien tech!
Watcha doin' Quent?
Proving my theory, Wade.
This is an electro magnetic pulse emitter.
Beep!
Beep!

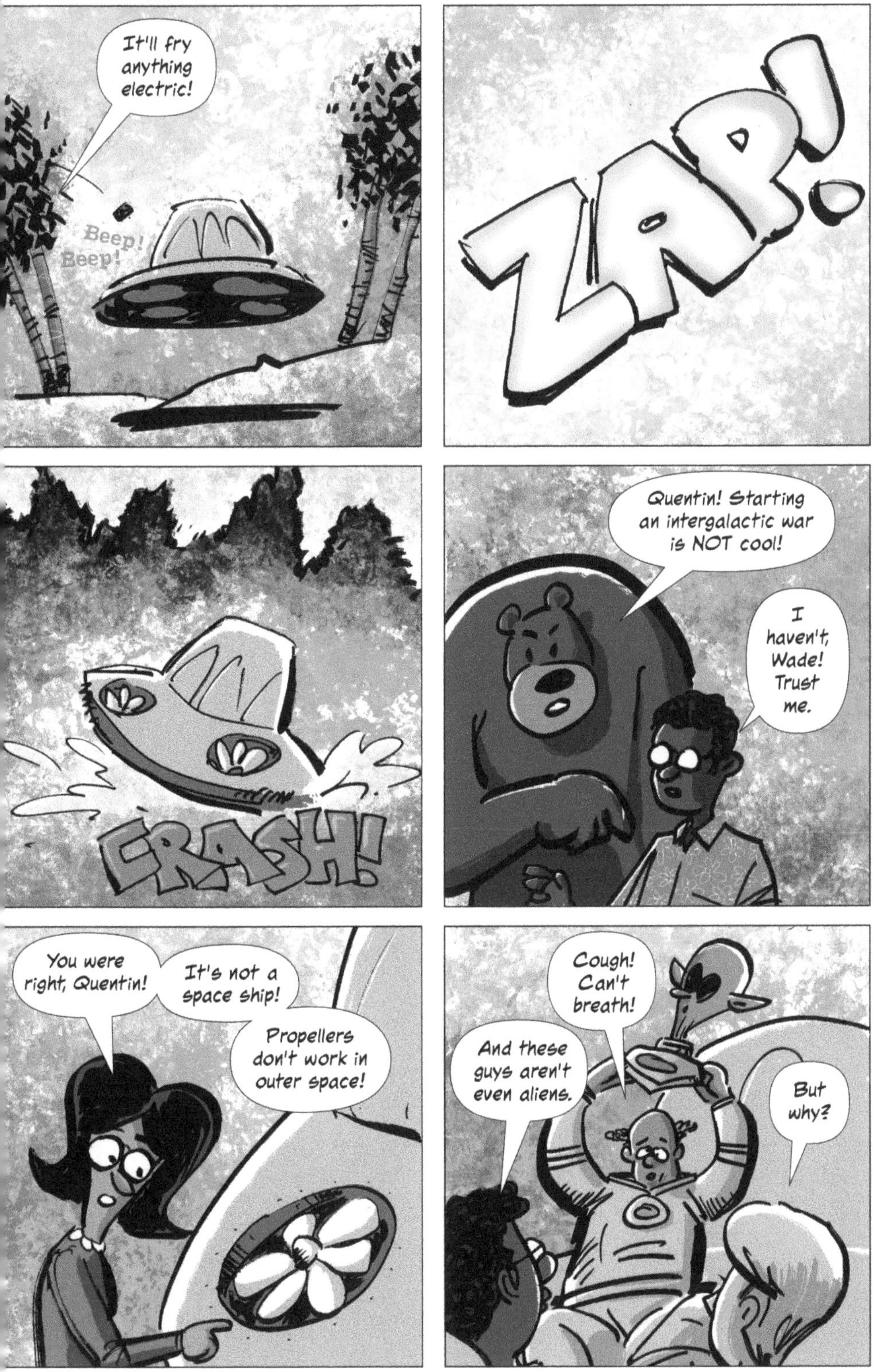
It'll fry anything electric!
Beep! Beep!
ZAP!
CRASH!
Quentin! Starting an intergalactic war is NOT cool!
I haven't, Wade! Trust me.
You were right, Quentin!
It's not a space ship!
Propellers don't work in outer space!
Cough! Can't breath!
And these guys aren't even aliens.
But why?

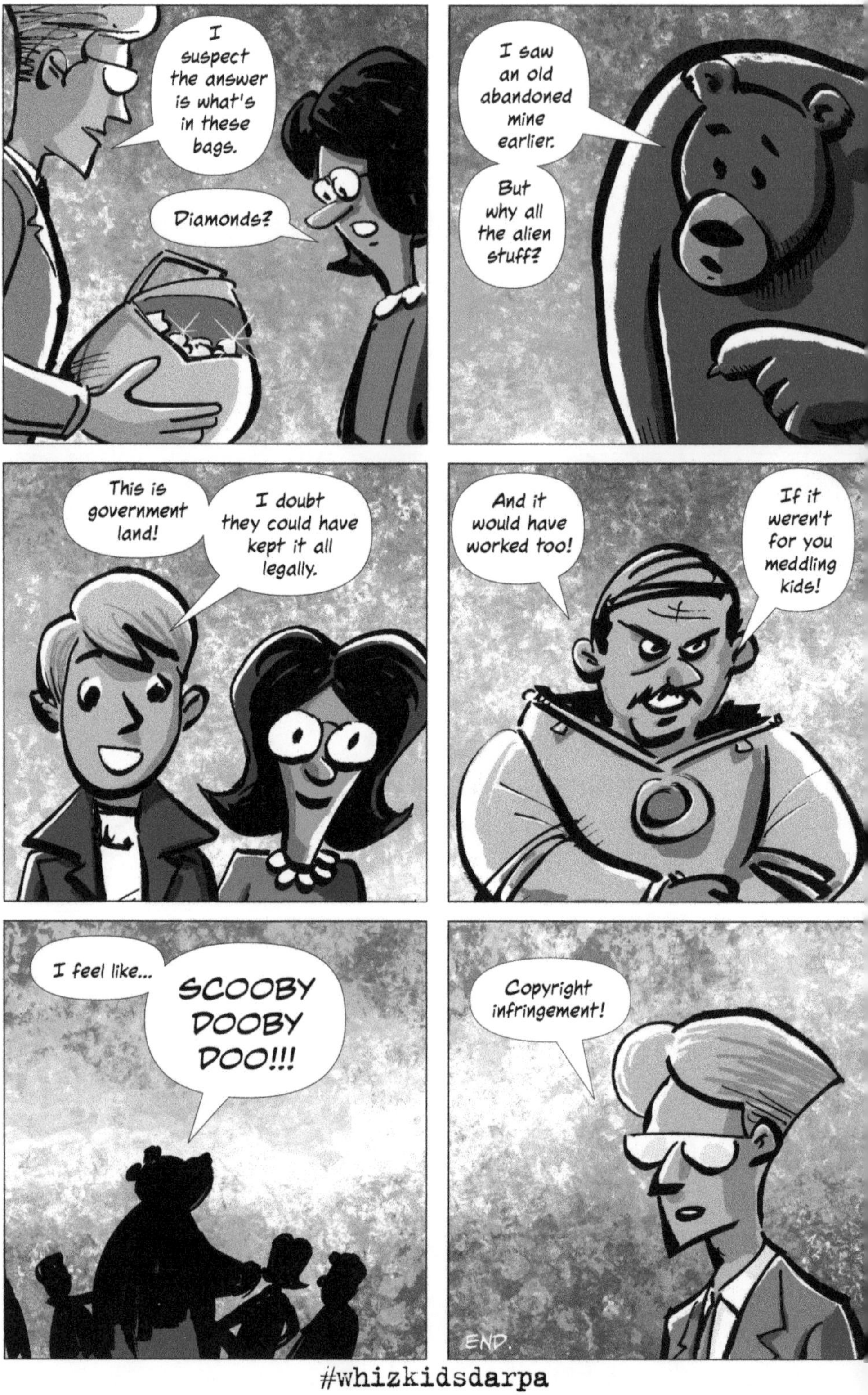
I suspect the answer is what's in these bags.
Diamonds?
I saw an old abandoned mine earlier.
But why all the alien stuff?
This is government land!
I doubt they could have kept it all legally.
And it would have worked too!
If it weren't for you meddling kids!
I feel like...
SCOOBY DOOBY DOO!!!
Copyright infringement!
END.

#whizkidsdarpa

Science Check

Propellers

Originally taken from a rotating screw design created by ancient Greek philosopher Archimedes, in the mid-1400s Leonardo DaVinci reused these designs in sketches for his first helicopter designs. By the mid-1700s propellers were being used to push ships through water. Soon, propellers were used in the first airships in combination with steam engines to power them. Finally, the Wright brothers invented the first airplane with "props." The spinning of these propellers shaped as wings displaced air or water backward to produce a forward thrust. But without air or water, like in outer space, they will not work.

For more information:
http://www.whizkidsdarpa.com/propellers

Extra-terrestrials

Meaning "Not from Earth," when people think of extra-terrestrials, they are thinking of aliens from other planets like in science fiction movies or TV shows. But extra-terrestrials can be microbes, bacteria, insects, plants as well as actual beings who walk and talk. They just have to be from anywhere but our planet. To date, scientists have not detected any proof of life from other planets or outer space but many people believe the odds are high that they exist. Some point to sightings of Unidentified Flying Objects (UFOs) as evidence of their existence but most of these reports are inconclusive.

For more information:
http://www.whizkidsdarpa.com/aliens

Chapter Six:
Hit The Road, Jack

Bad wheather threatens the safety of the team
during a trip to research, well...bad weather.

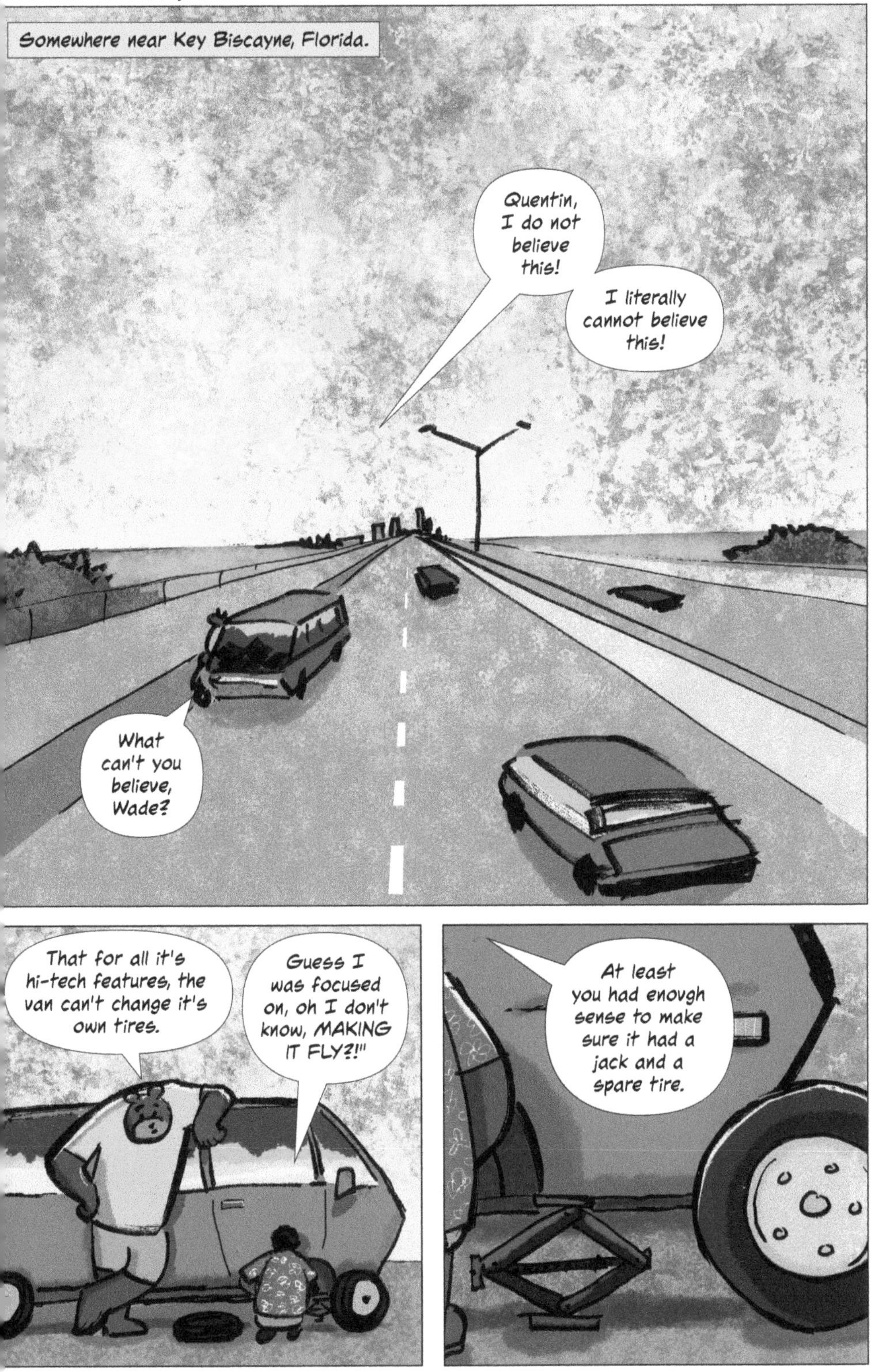
Somewhere near Key Biscayne, Florida.
Quentin, I do not believe this!
I literally cannot believe this!
What can't you believe, Wade?
That for all it's hi-tech features, the van can't change it's own tires.
Guess I was focused on, oh I don't know, MAKING IT FLY?!"
At least you had enough sense to make sure it had a jack and a spare tire.

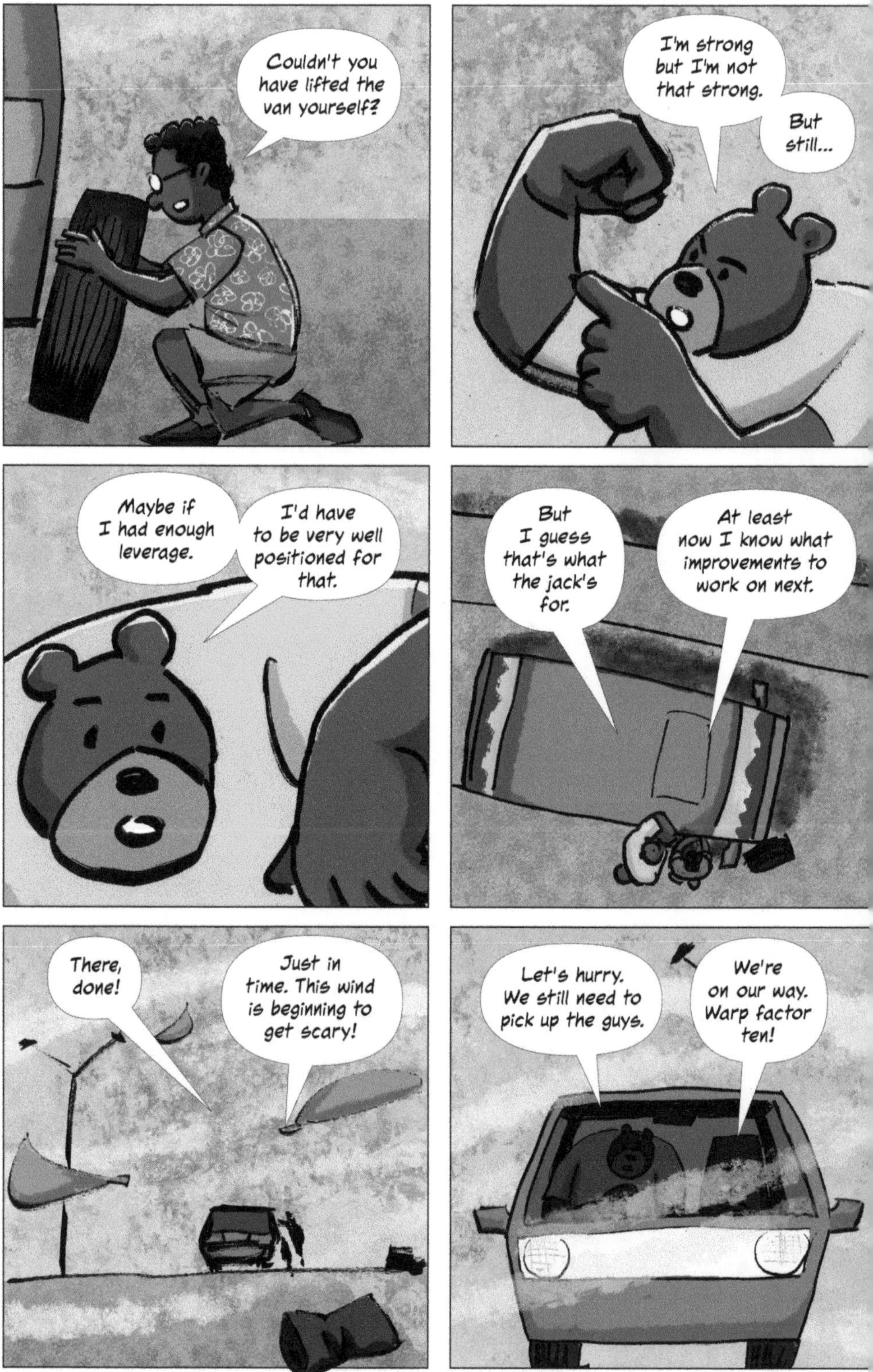
Couldn't you have lifted the van yourself?
I'm strong but I'm not that strong.
But still...
Maybe if I had enough leverage.
I'd have to be very well positioned for that.
But I guess that's what the jack's for.
At least now I know what improvements to work on next.
There, done!
Just in time. This wind is beginning to get scary!
Let's hurry. We still need to pick up the guys.
We're on our way. Warp factor ten!

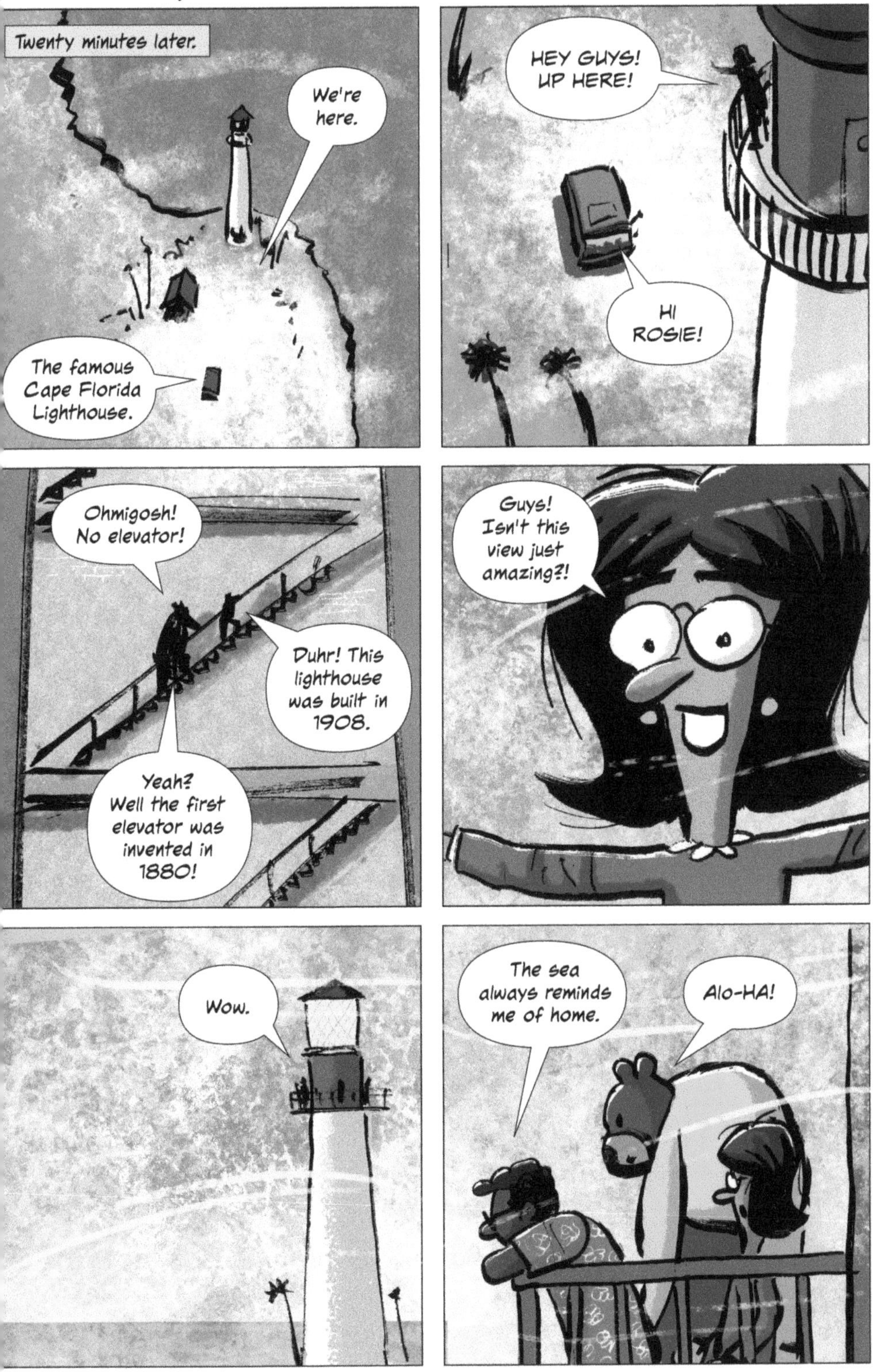
Twenty minutes later.
We're here.
The famous Cape Florida Lighthouse.
HEY GUYS! UP HERE!
HI ROSIE!
Ohmigosh! No elevator!
Duhr! This lighthouse was built in 1908.
Yeah? Well the first elevator was invented in 1880!
Guys! Isn't this view just amazing?!
Wow.
The sea always reminds me of home.
Alo-HA!

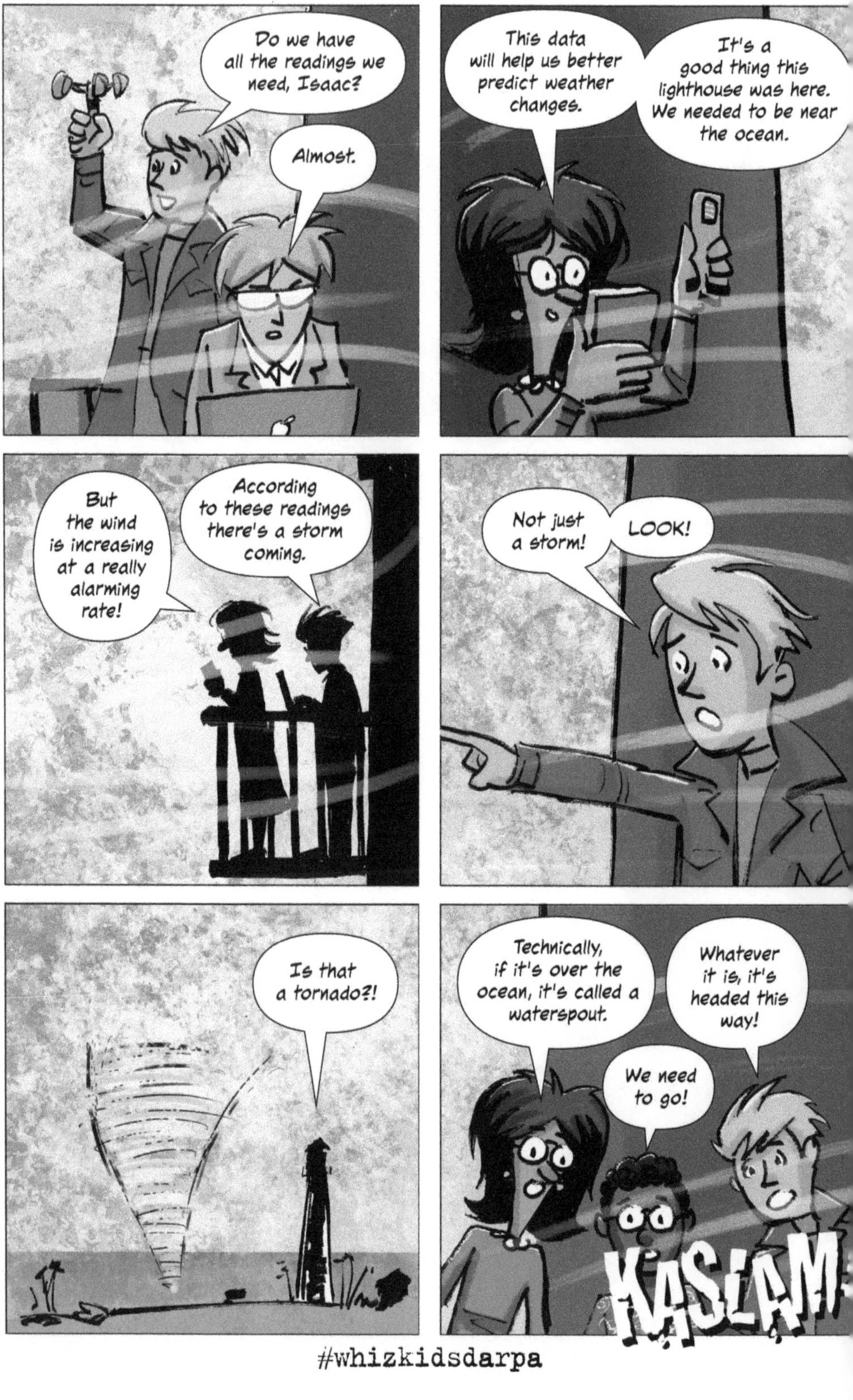
Do we have all the readings we need, Isaac?
Almost.
This data will help us better predict weather changes.
It's a good thing this lighthouse was here. We needed to be near the ocean.
But the wind is increasing at a really alarming rate!
According to these readings there's a storm coming.
Not just a storm!
LOOK!
Is that a tornado?!
Technically, if it's over the ocean, it's called a waterspout.
Whatever it is, it's headed this way!
We need to go!
KASLAM

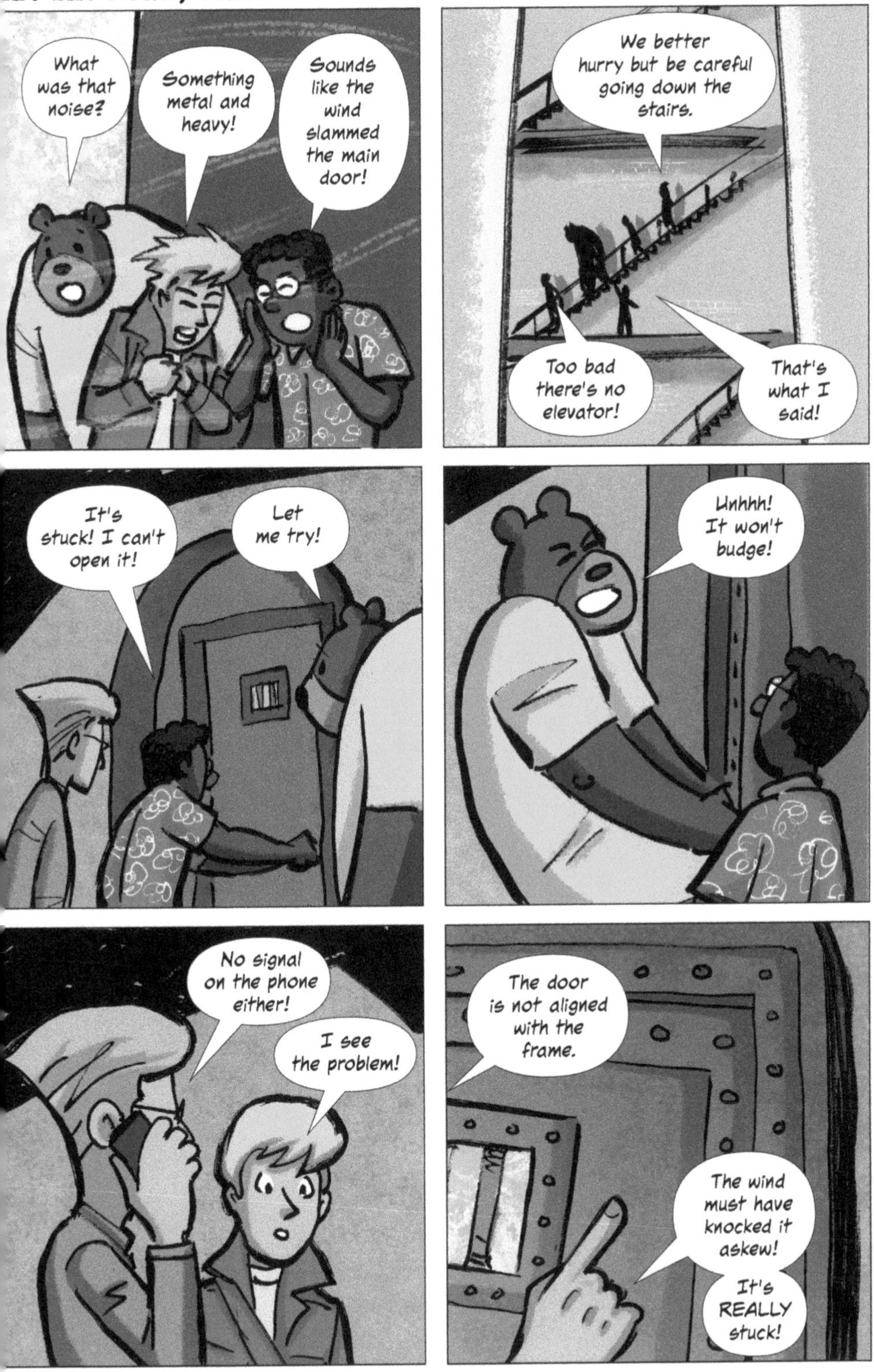
What was that noise?
Something metal and heavy!
Sounds like the wind slammed the main door!
We better hurry but be careful going down the stairs.
Too bad there's no elevator!
That's what I said!
It's stuck! I can't open it!
Let me try!
Unhhh! It won't budge!
No signal on the phone either!
I see the problem!
The door is not aligned with the frame.
The wind must have knocked it askew!
It's REALLY stuck!

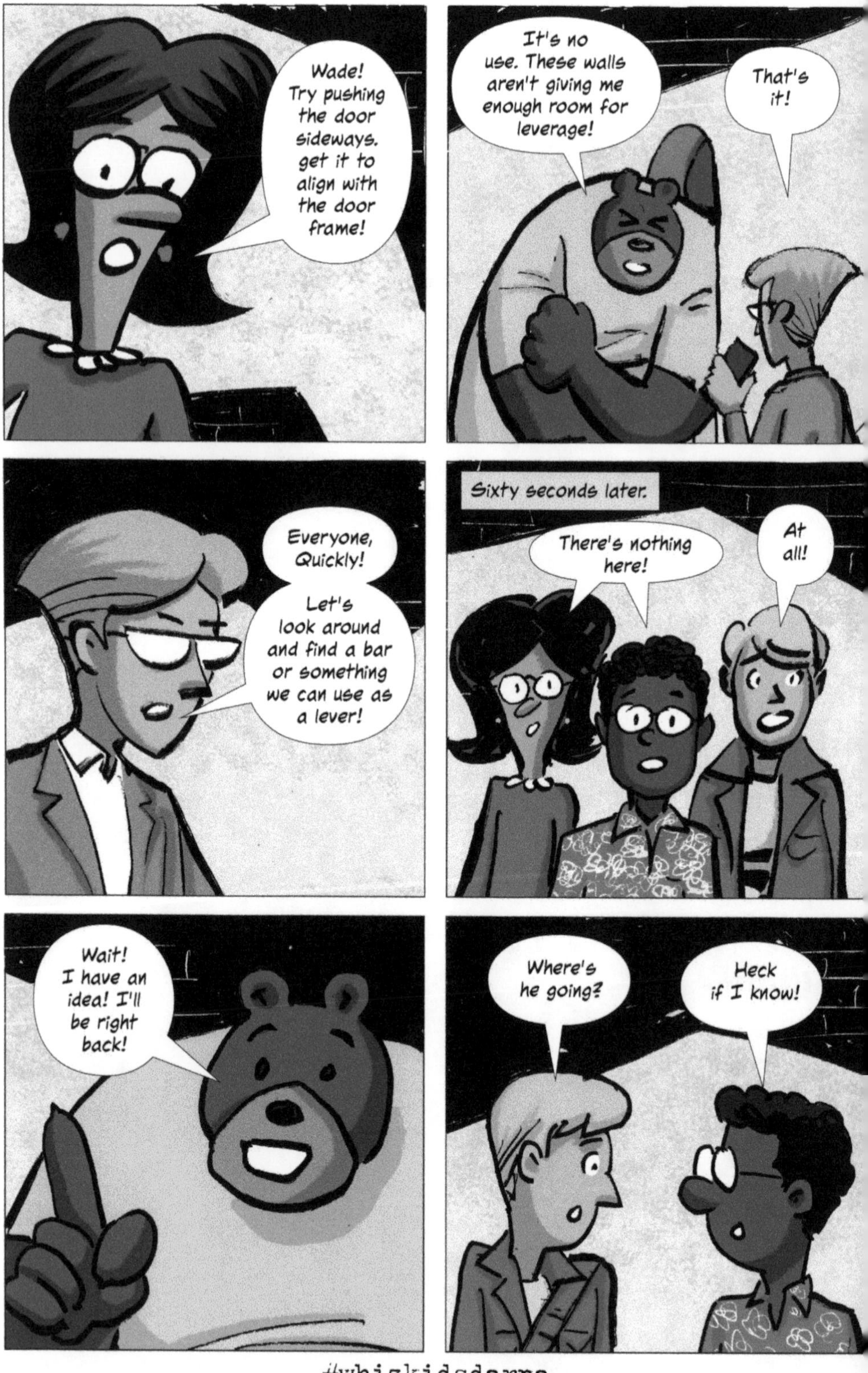
Wade! Try pushing the door sideways. get it to align with the door frame!
It's no use. These walls aren't giving me enough room for leverage!
That's it!
Everyone, Quickly!
Let's look around and find a bar or something we can use as a lever!
Sixty seconds later.
There's nothing here!
At all!
Wait! I have an idea! I'll be right back!
Where's he going?
Heck if I know!

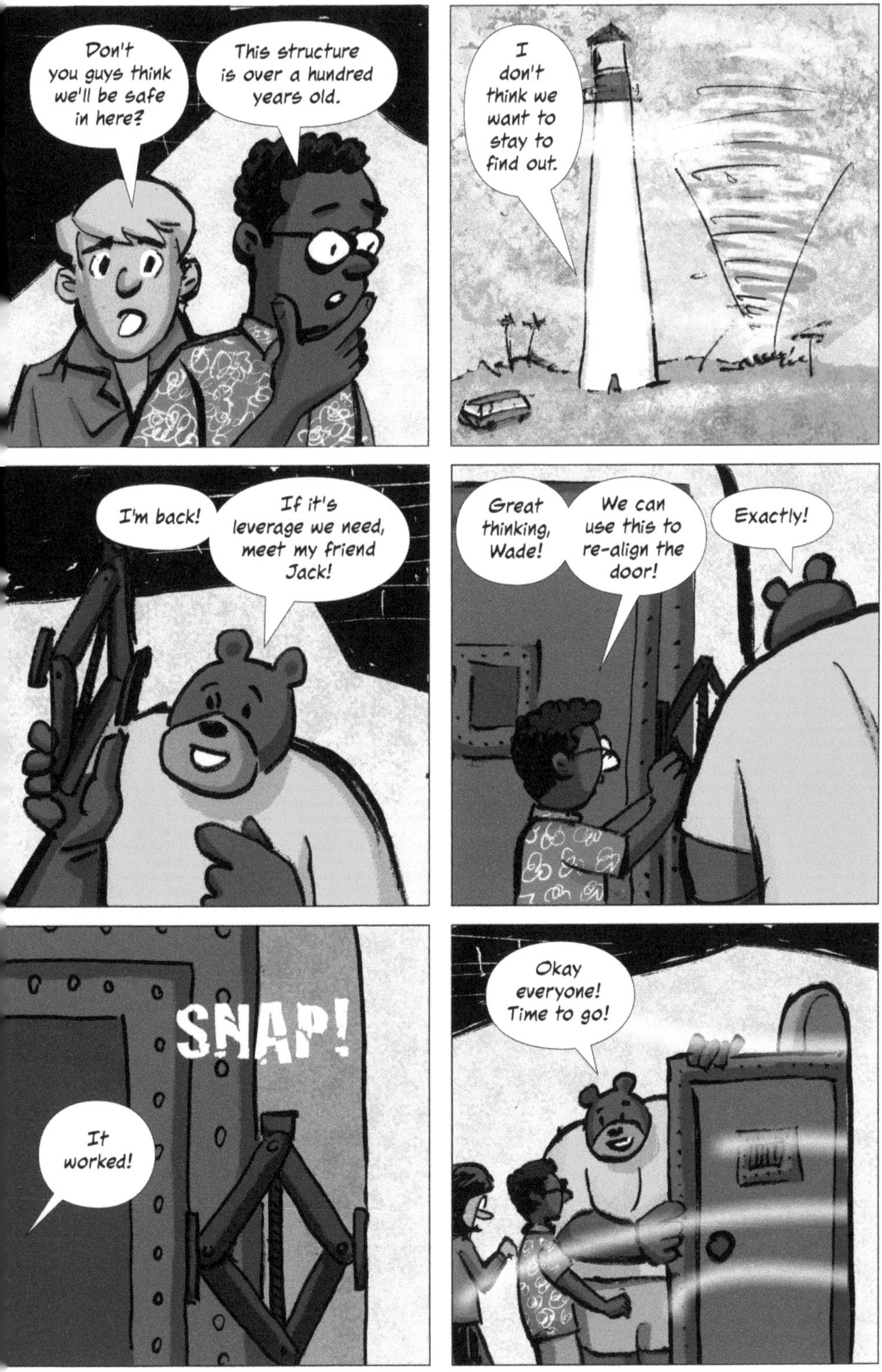
Don't you guys think we'll be safe in here?
This structure is over a hundred years old.
I don't think we want to stay to find out.
I'm back!
If it's leverage we need, meet my friend Jack!
Great thinking, Wade!
We can use this to re-align the door!
Exactly!
SNAP!
It worked!
Okay everyone! Time to go!

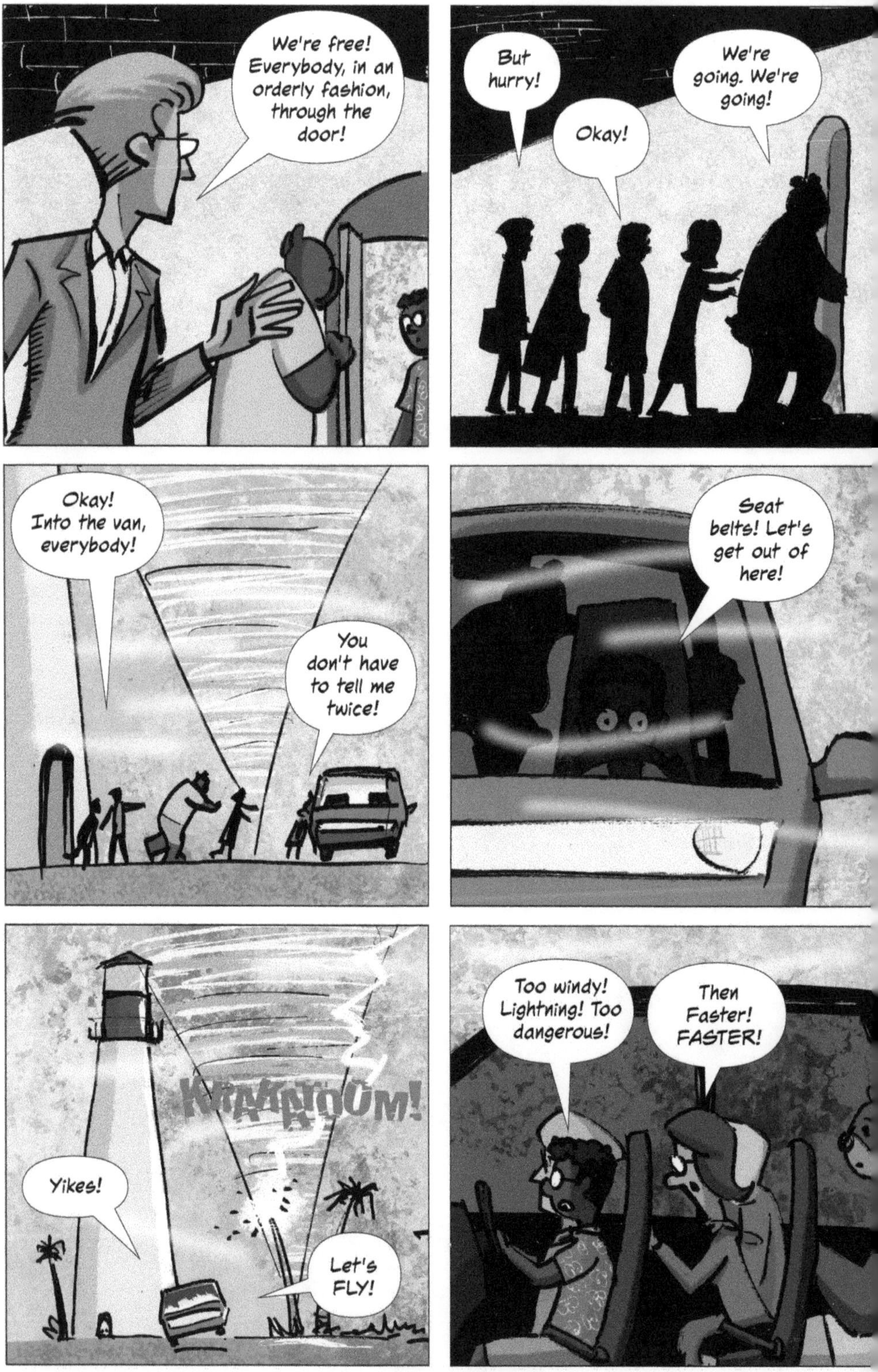
We're free! Everybody, in an orderly fashion, through the door!
But hurry!
Okay!
We're going. We're going!
Okay! Into the van, everybody!
You don't have to tell me twice!
Seat belts! Let's get out of here!
KRAKATOOM!
Yikes!
Let's FLY!
Too windy! Lightning! Too dangerous!
Then Faster! FASTER!

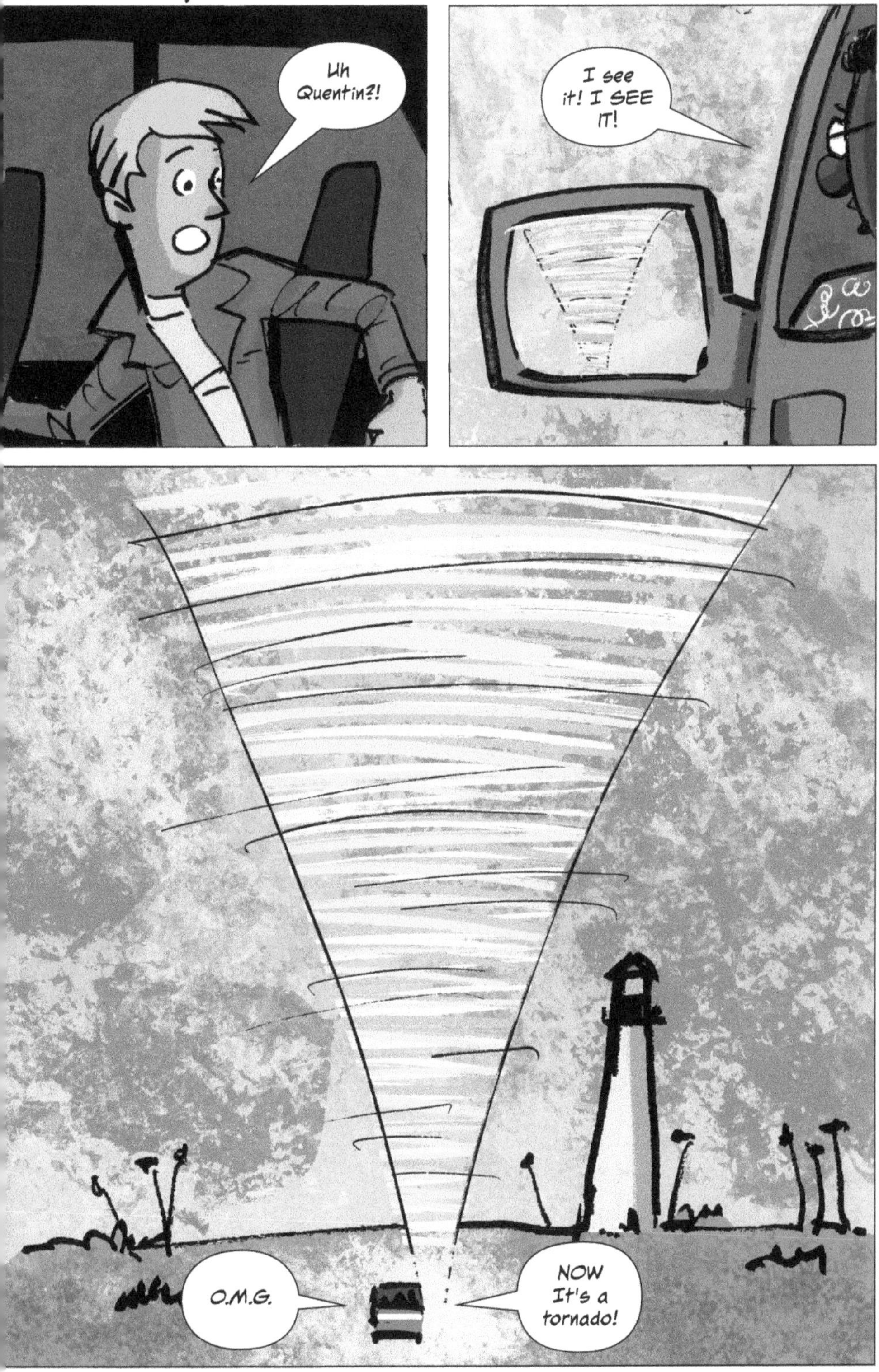
Uh Quentin?!
I see it! I SEE IT!
O.M.G.
NOW It's a tornado!

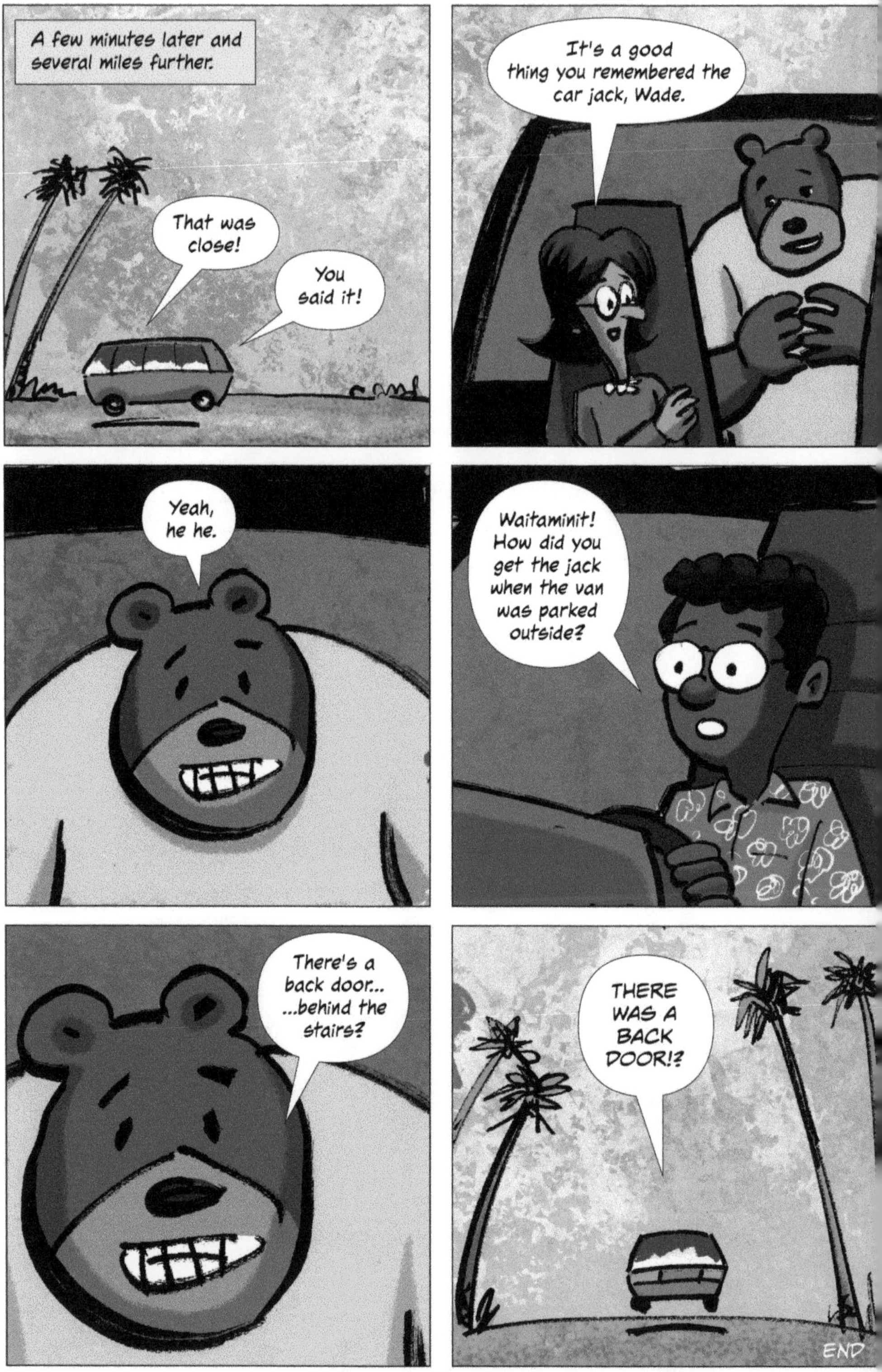
A few minutes later and several miles further.
That was close!
You said it!
It's a good thing you remembered the car jack, Wade.
Yeah, he he.
Waitaminit! How did you get the jack when the van was parked outside?
There's a back door... ...behind the stairs?
THERE WAS A BACK DOOR!?
END

Science Check

Tornadoes and Waterspouts

Tornadoes happen when strong winds coming from different directions meet and form incredibly strong spinning gusts of air that can go over 150 miles per hour. Strong enough to blow away cars, trees, houses and people. When tornadoes happen over water, they are called waterspouts. Both tornadoes and waterspouts often come with rainstorms, thunder and lightning.

For more information:
http://www.whizkidsdarpa.com/waterspouts

Car Jacks

When you rotate the screw on a scissors-style car jack, each turn creates a tiny amount of force that can be used to push up a heavy object a little bit at a time. As the screw turns, it moves the nuts of two levers, bringing them closer together and thus making the jack taller and taller as their angles thrust upwards. This allows a person with normal strength to lift something like a car in tiny increments.

For more information:
http://www.whizkidsdarpa.com/carjack

Chapter Seven:

Quentin

Quentin talks to a friend regarding his fears
about going after his dreams.

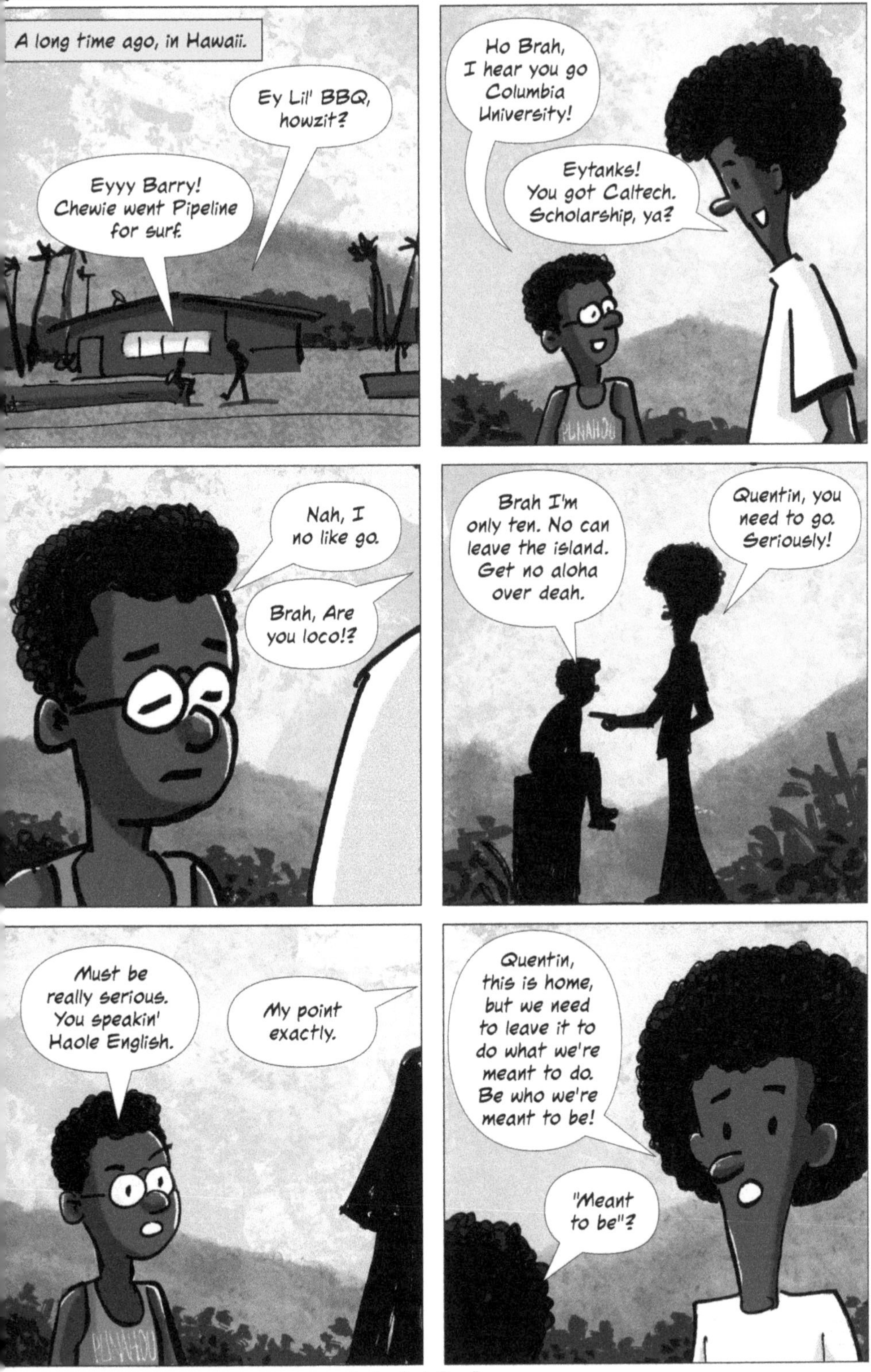
A long time ago, in Hawaii.
Ey Lil' BBQ, howzit?
Eyyy Barry! Chewie went Pipeline for surf.
Ho Brah, I hear you go Columbia University!
Eytanks! You got Caltech. Scholarship, ya?
Nah, I no like go.
Brah, Are you loco!?
Brah I'm only ten. No can leave the island. Get no aloha over deah.
Quentin, you need to go. Seriously!
Must be really serious. You speakin' Haole English.
My point exactly.
Quentin, this is home, but we need to leave it to do what we're meant to do. Be who we're meant to be!
"Meant to be"?

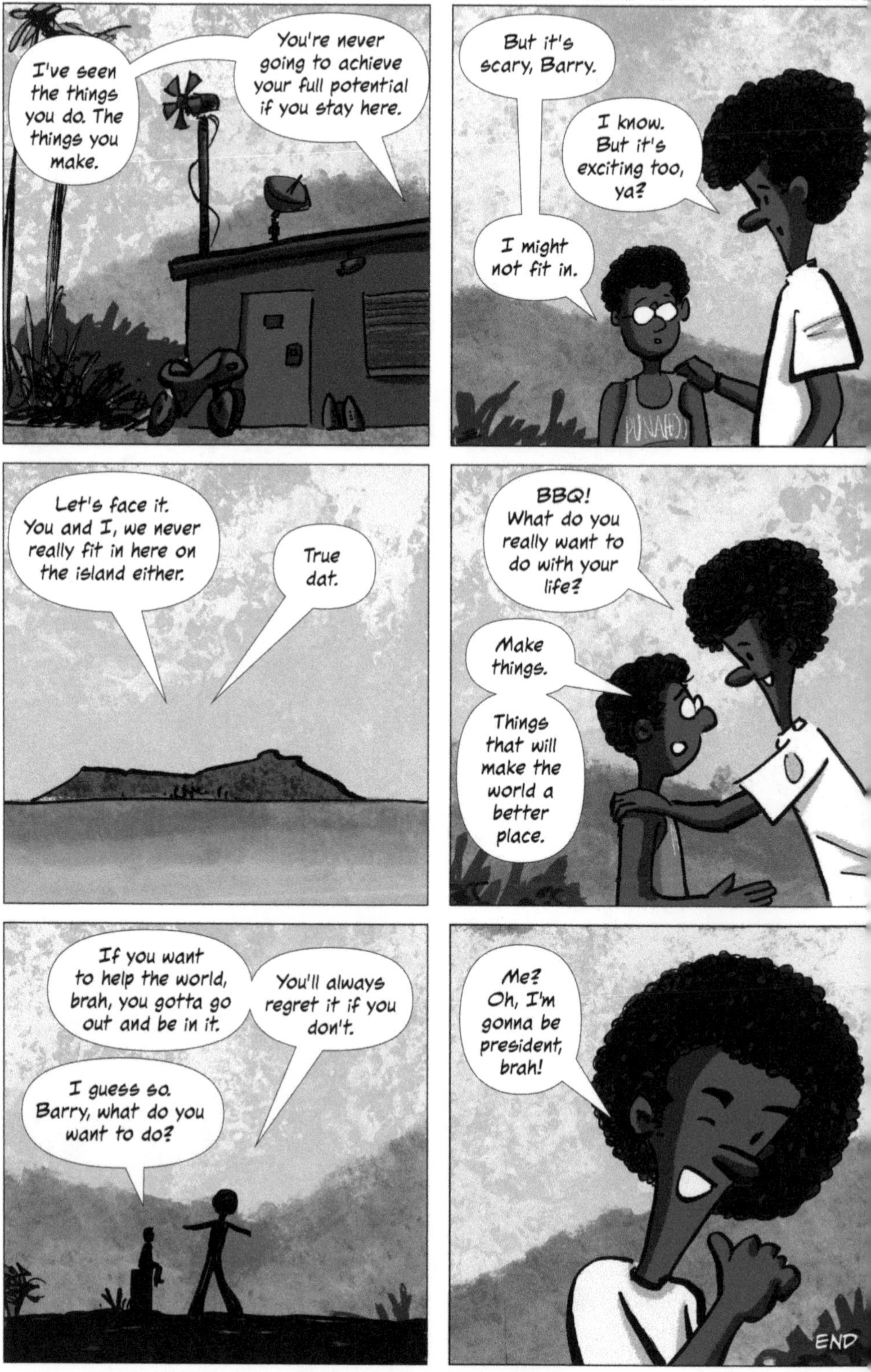
I've seen the things you do. The things you make.
You're never going to achieve your full potential if you stay here.
But it's scary, Barry.
I know. But it's exciting too, ya?
I might not fit in.
Let's face it. You and I, we never really fit in here on the island either.
True dat.
BBQ! What do you really want to do with your life?
Make things.
Things that will make the world a better place.
If you want to help the world, brah, you gotta go out and be in it.
You'll always regret it if you don't.
I guess so. Barry, what do you want to do?
Me? Oh, I'm gonna be president, brah!
END

Science Check

Goals

Many people have goals and ambitions for themselves. Sometimes they want to do the same work their parents do and sometimes they want to do something else entirely. Depending on the goal, it could mean leaving your hometown or even your home state or country. Sometimes you need to get more education like college or from a specialized school. Goals are often based on things we love to do or care for or dream about. The bigger a goal, the more effort is usually required. The question one must ask is "How badly enough do you want it?"

For more information:
http://www.whizkidsdarpa.com/goals

Scholarships

Schools and colleges often give out scholarships to students who want to attend their institution. This means being able to go to that school for free or at least have some or most of the tuition paid for. Scholarships are often based on being really good at something. Having good grades in general or a specific subject or being good at a sport or activity. Some scholarships are simply given to students who might not be able to afford a school otherwise. But good grades always help. Just ask your teacher.

For more information:
http://www.whizkidsdarpa.com/scholarships

Chapter Eight:

Finding Nemo

The U.S. Space Force once again enlists the aid of the Whiz Kids in recovering some top secret hardware.

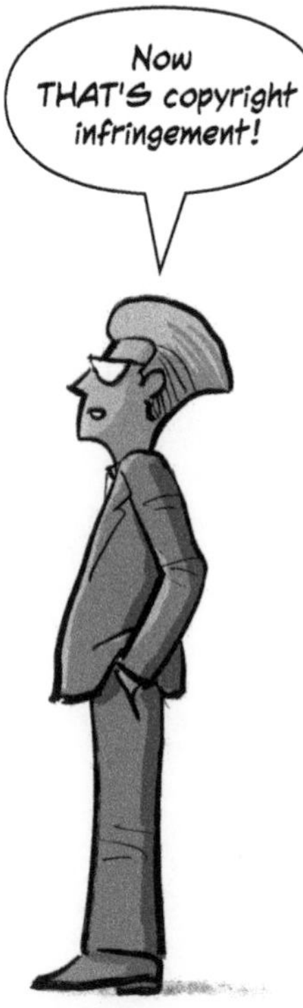
Now THAT'S copyright infringement!

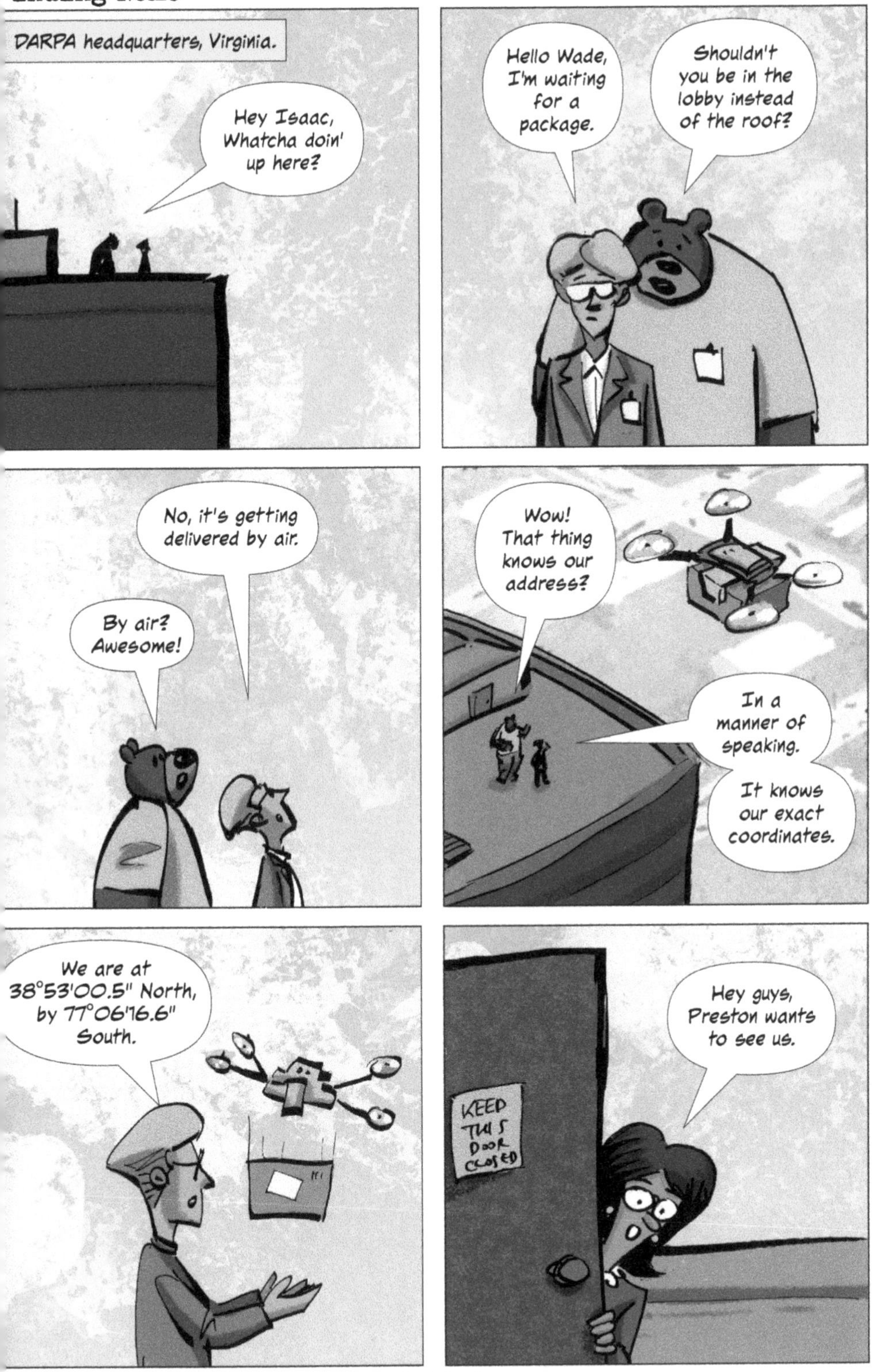
DARPA headquarters, Virginia.
Hey Isaac, Whatcha doin' up here?
Hello Wade, I'm waiting for a package.
Shouldn't you be in the lobby instead of the roof?
No, it's getting delivered by air.
By air? Awesome!
Wow! That thing knows our address?
In a manner of speaking.
It knows our exact coordinates.
We are at 38°53'00.5" North, by 77°06'16.6" South.
Hey guys, Preston wants to see us.
KEEP THIS DOOR CLOSED

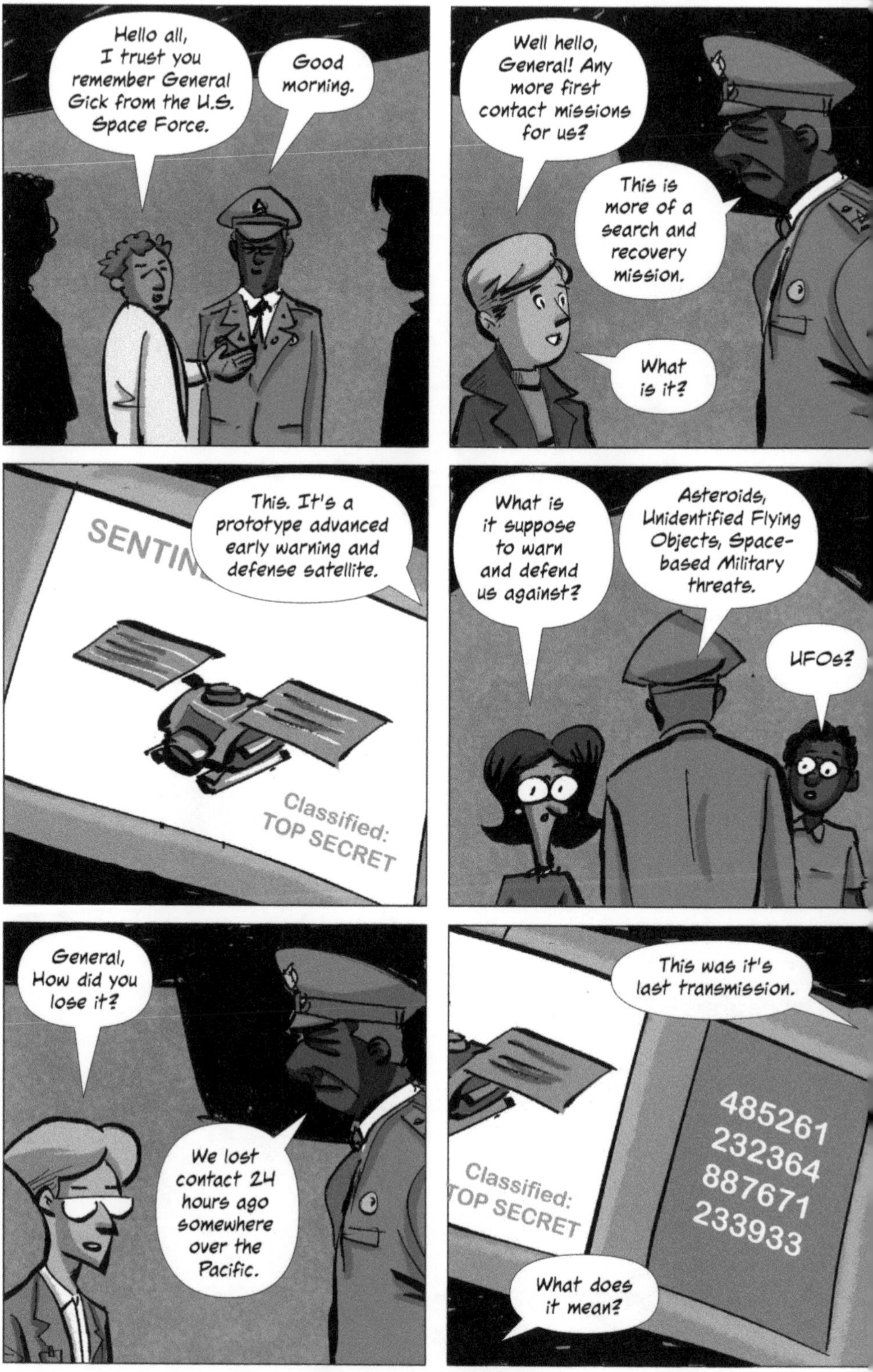
Hello all, I trust you remember General Gick from the U.S. Space Force.
Good morning.
Well hello, General! Any more first contact missions for us?
This is more of a search and recovery mission.
What is it?
This. It's a prototype advanced early warning and defense satellite.
SENTIN
Classified: TOP SECRET
What is it suppose to warn and defend us against?
Asteroids, Unidentified Flying Objects, Space-based Military threats.
UFOs?
General, How did you lose it?
We lost contact 24 hours ago somewhere over the Pacific.
This was it's last transmission.
Classified: TOP SECRET
485261
232364
887671
233933
What does it mean?

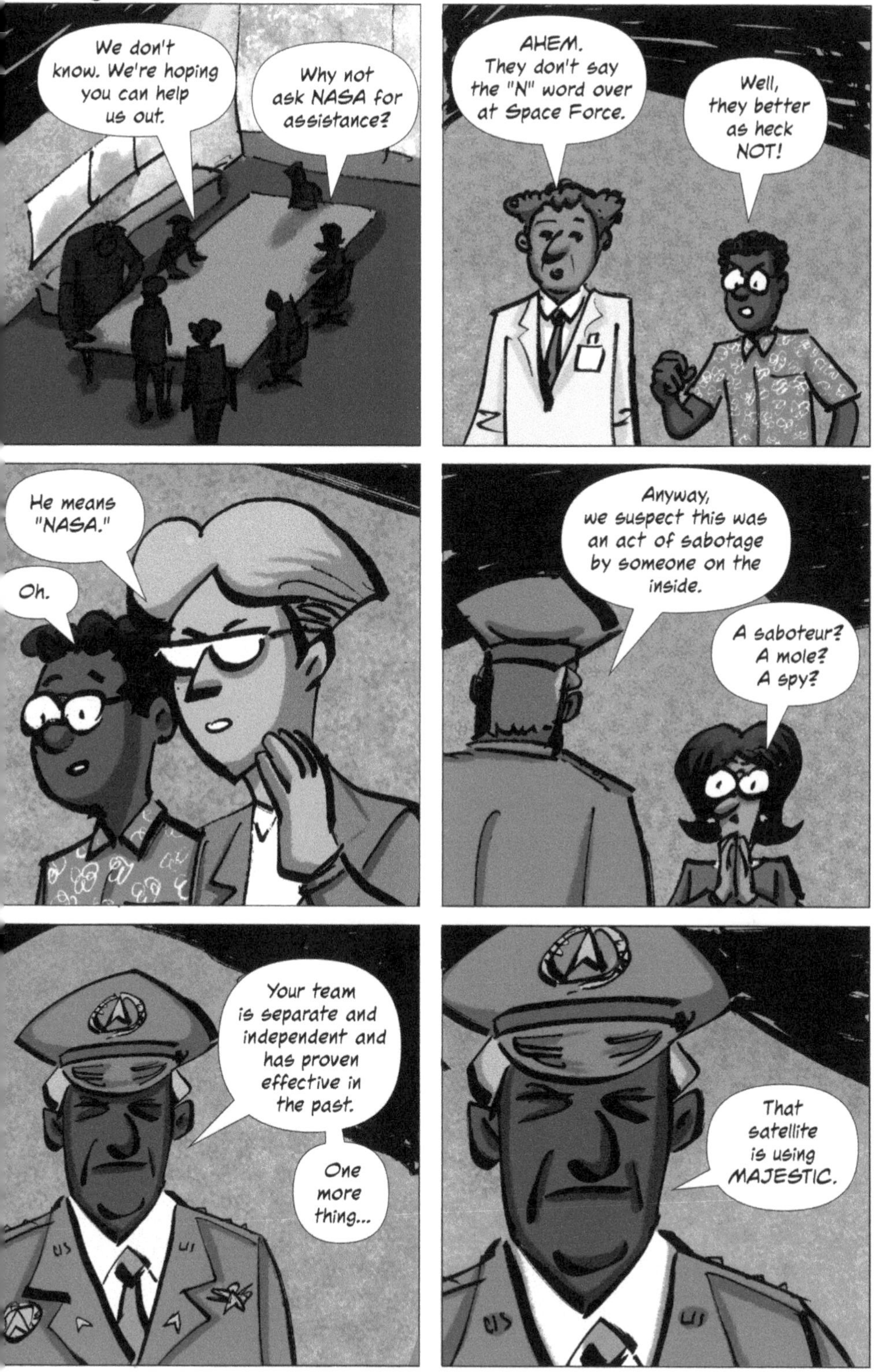
We don't know. We're hoping you can help us out.
Why not ask NASA for assistance?
AHEM. They don't say the "N" word over at Space Force.
Well, they better as heck NOT!
He means "NASA."
Oh.
Anyway, we suspect this was an act of sabotage by someone on the inside.
A saboteur? A mole? A spy?
Your team is separate and independent and has proven effective in the past.
One more thing...
That satellite is using MAJESTIC.

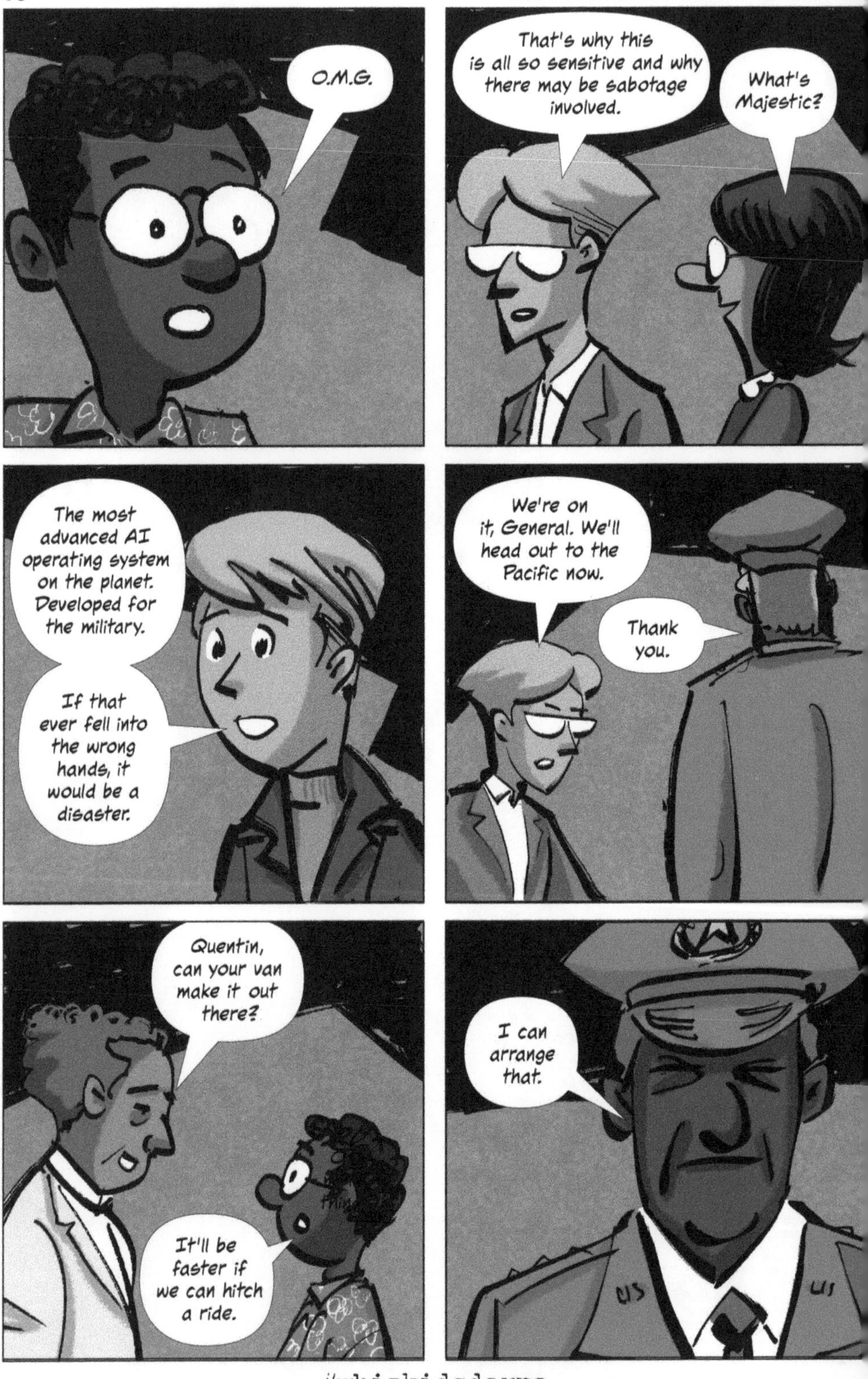
O.M.G.
That's why this is all so sensitive and why there may be sabotage involved.
What's Majestic?
The most advanced AI operating system on the planet. Developed for the military.
If that ever fell into the wrong hands, it would be a disaster.
We're on it, General. We'll head out to the Pacific now.
Thank you.
Quentin, can your van make it out there?
It'll be faster if we can hitch a ride.
I can arrange that.

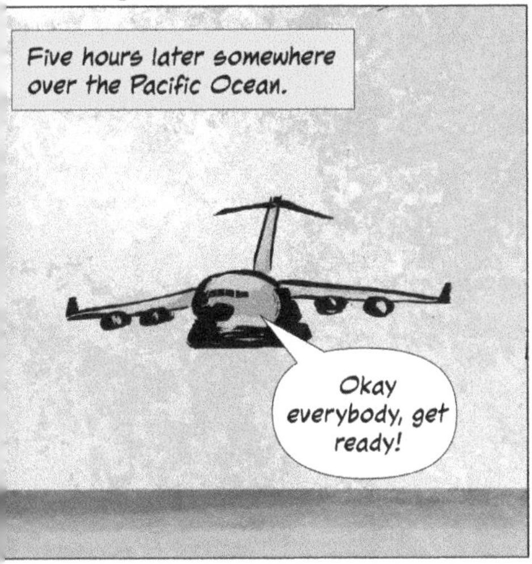
Five hours later somewhere over the Pacific Ocean.
Okay everybody, get ready!

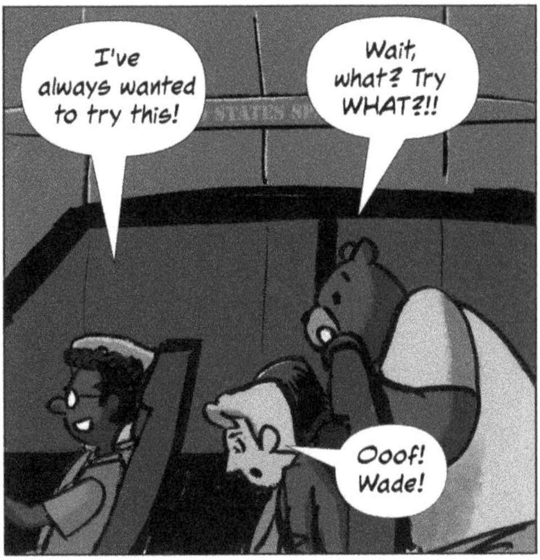
I've always wanted to try this!
Wait, what? Try WHAT?!!
Ooof! Wade!

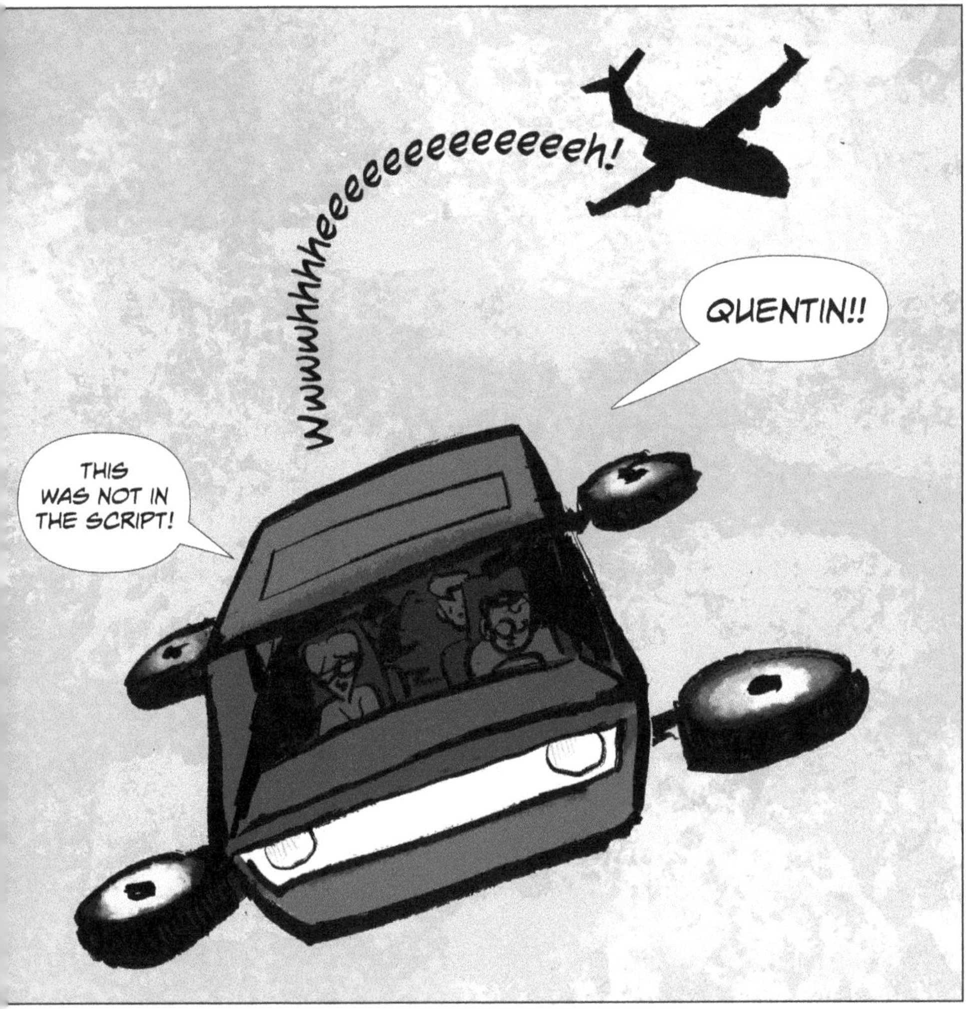
Wwwwwhhheeeeeeeeeeeeeeh!
QUENTIN!!
THIS WAS NOT IN THE SCRIPT!

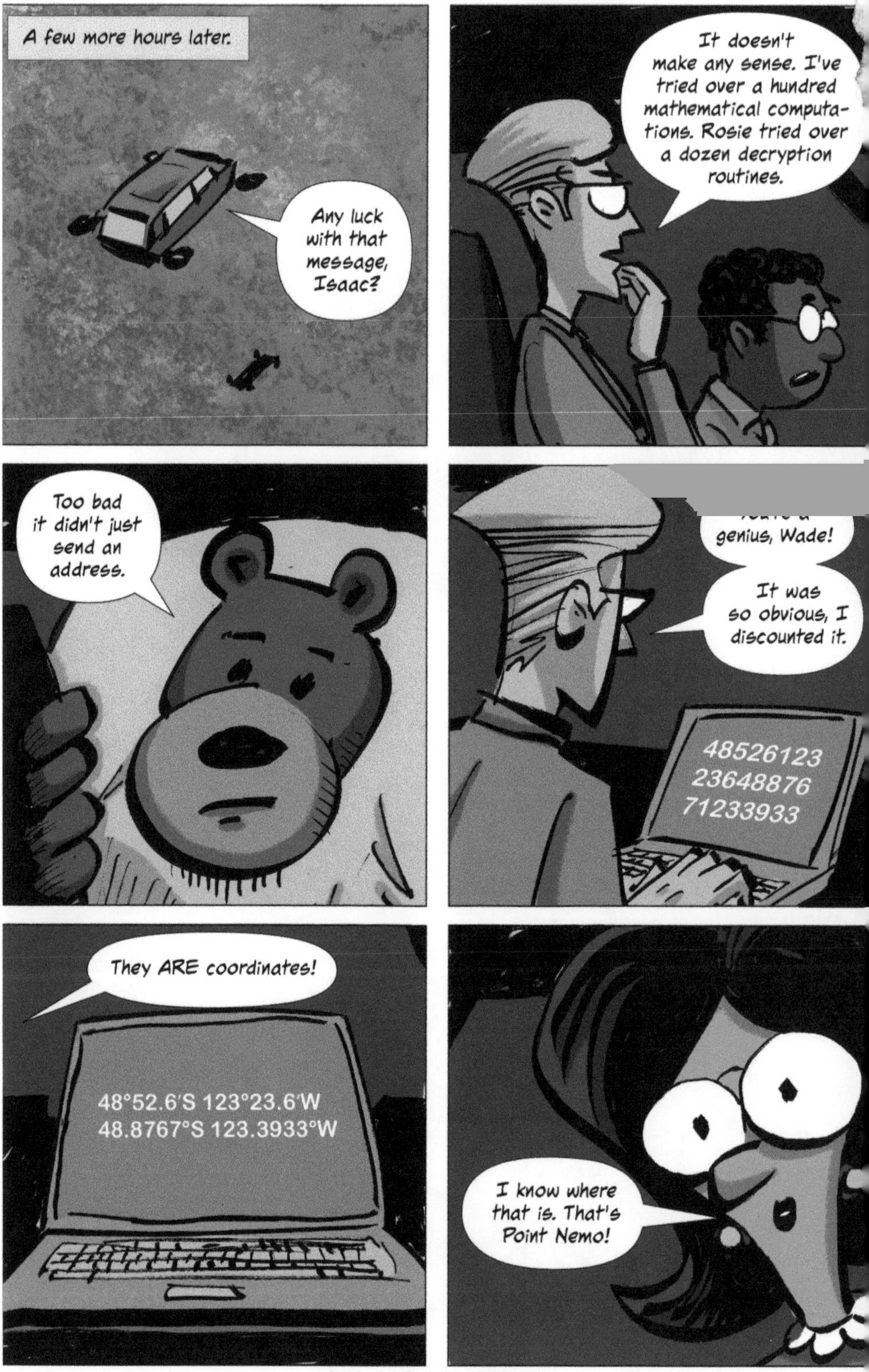

A few more hours later.
Any luck with that message, Isaac?
It doesn't make any sense. I've tried over a hundred mathematical computations. Rosie tried over a dozen decryption routines.
Too bad it didn't just send an address.
genius, Wade!
It was so obvious, I discounted it.
48526123
23648876
71233933
They ARE coordinates!
48°52.6′S 123°23.6′W
48.8767°S 123.3933°W
I know where that is. That's Point Nemo!

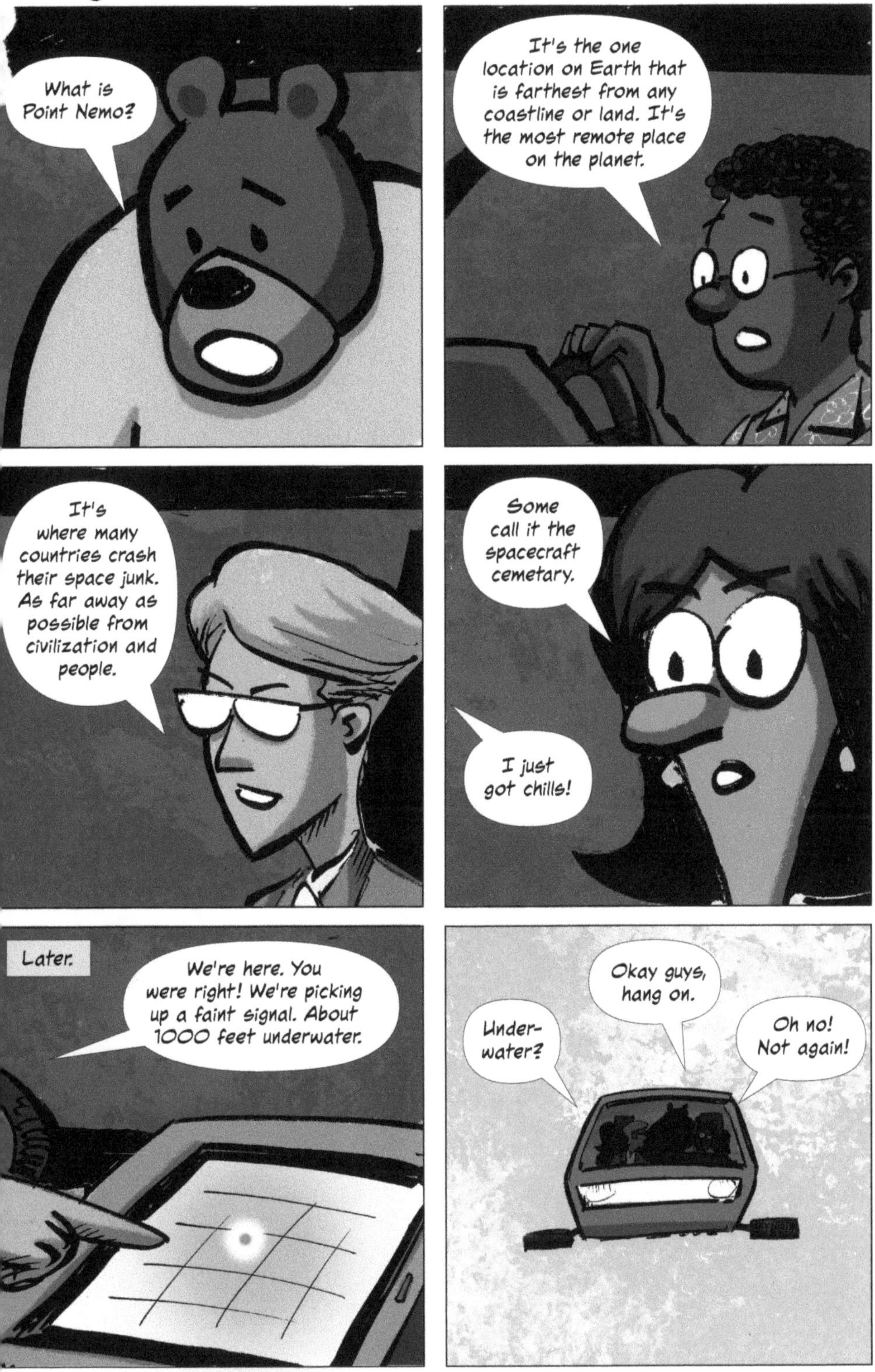
What is Point Nemo?
It's the one location on Earth that is farthest from any coastline or land. It's the most remote place on the planet.
It's where many countries crash their space junk. As far away as possible from civilization and people.
Some call it the spacecraft cemetary.
I just got chills!
Later.
We're here. You were right! We're picking up a faint signal. About 1000 feet underwater.
Under-water?
Okay guys, hang on.
Oh no! Not again!

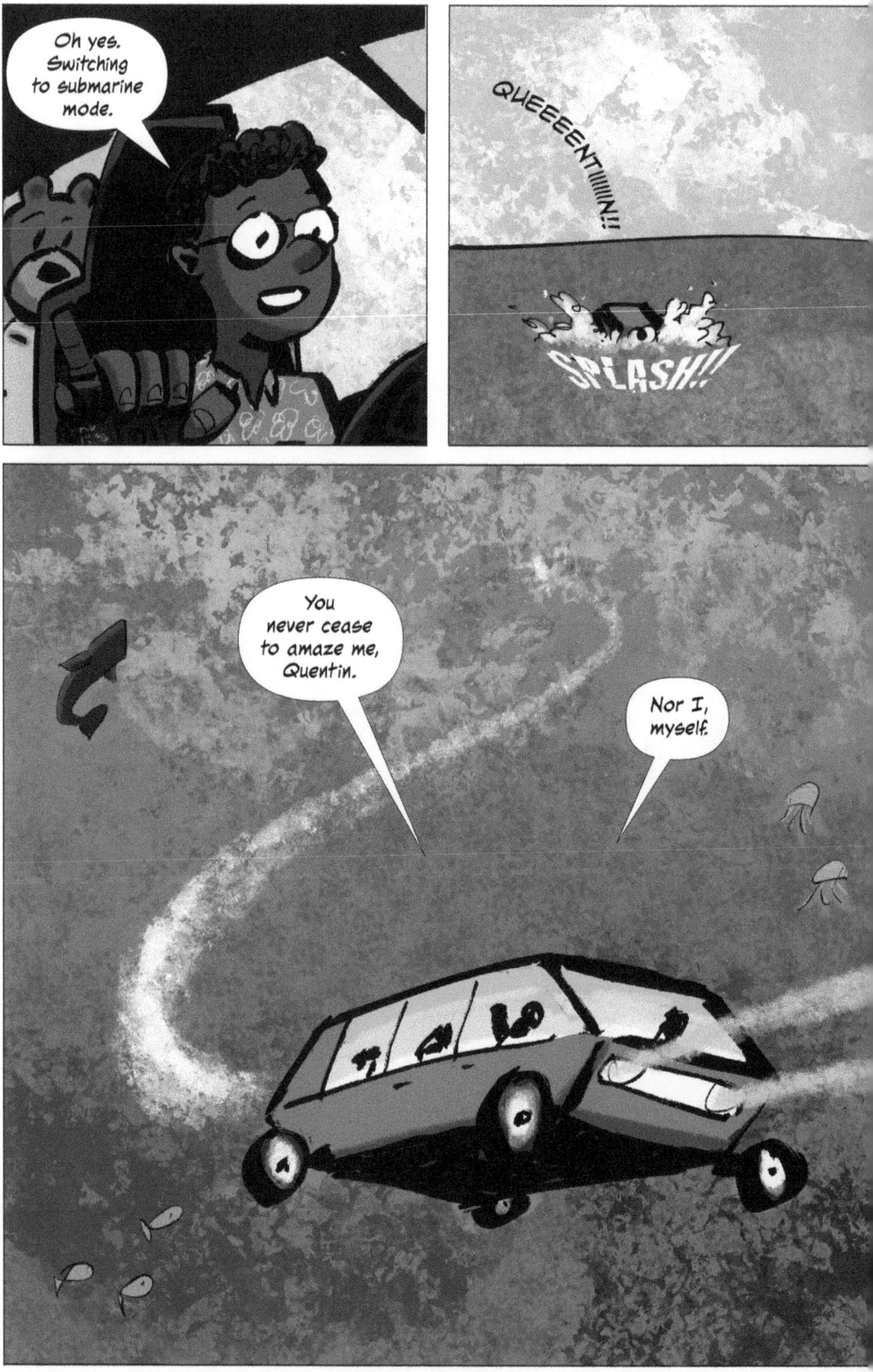
Oh yes. Switching to submarine mode.
QUEEEEENT!!!!!!N!!
SPLASH!!
You never cease to amaze me, Quentin.
Nor I, myself.

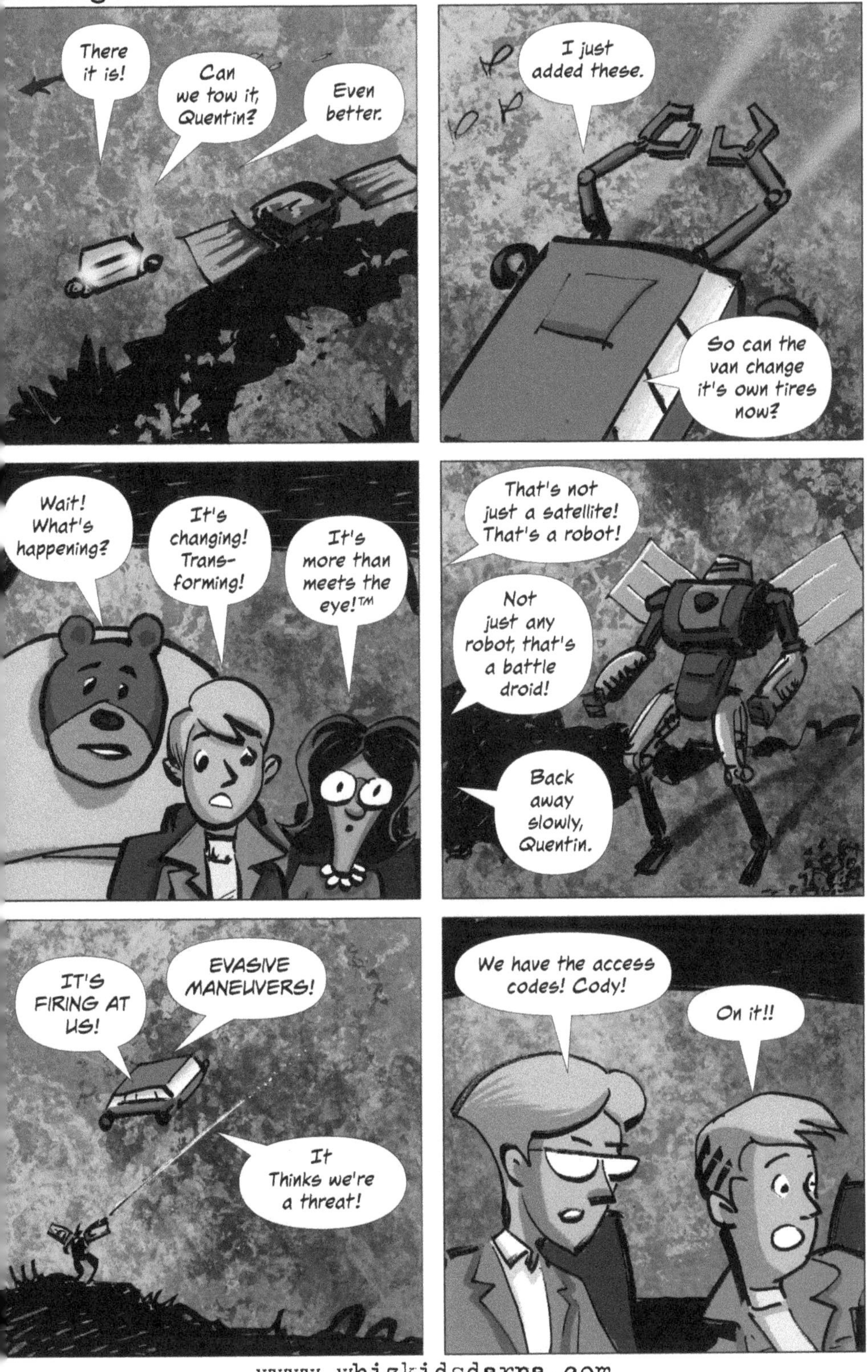
There it is!
Can we tow it, Quentin?
Even better.
I just added these.
So can the van change it's own tires now?
Wait! What's happening?
It's changing! Trans-forming!
It's more than meets the eye!™
That's not just a satellite! That's a robot!
Not just any robot, that's a battle droid!
Back away slowly, Quentin.
IT'S FIRING AT US!
EVASIVE MANEUVERS!
It Thinks we're a threat!
We have the access codes! Cody!
On it!!

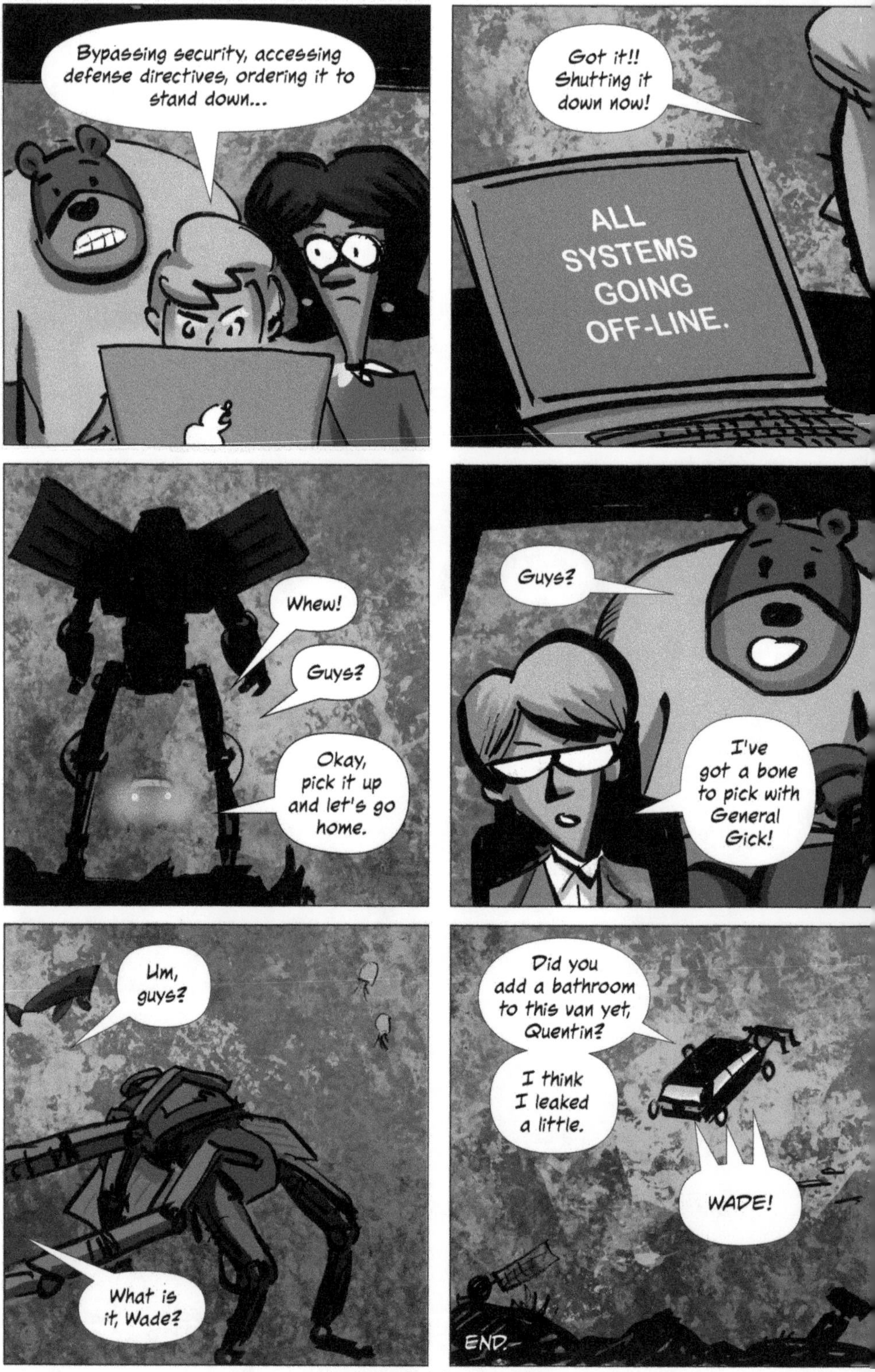
Bypassing security, accessing defense directives, ordering it to stand down...
Got it!! Shutting it down now!
ALL SYSTEMS GOING OFF-LINE.
Whew!
Guys?
Okay, pick it up and let's go home.
Guys?
I've got a bone to pick with General Gick!
Um, guys?
What is it, Wade?
Did you add a bathroom to this van yet, Quentin?
I think I leaked a little.
WADE!
END.

#whizkidsdarpa

Science Check

Satellites

Objects that orbit a large body in space are called satellites. The moon is a satellite of Earth. The first man-made satellite, Sputnik 1, was launched in 1957. Since then, space agencies and private companies have sent satellites into orbit for communication, weather prediction, spying and even to live in. The International Space Station, Mir and Skylab are considered satellites.

For more information:
http://www.whizkidsdarpa.com/satellites

Point Nemo

Named after the anti-social and mysterious Captain Nemo of Jules Verne's book *20,000 Leagues Under the Sea*, Point Nemo is the most isolated and remote place on the planet. It is in the middle of the Pacific Ocean and the closest coast is almost 3000 kilometers away. Because of this remoteness, many space agencies choose this spot to "crash" their decommissioned space junk like old satellites and booster rockets. Hence it often called "The Spacecraft Cemetery."

For more information:
http://www.whizkidsdarpa.com/pointnemo

Chapter Nine:

A Day at the Zoo

With the help of Rosie, Wade tries to communicate
with his fellow non-humans through the use body chemistry.

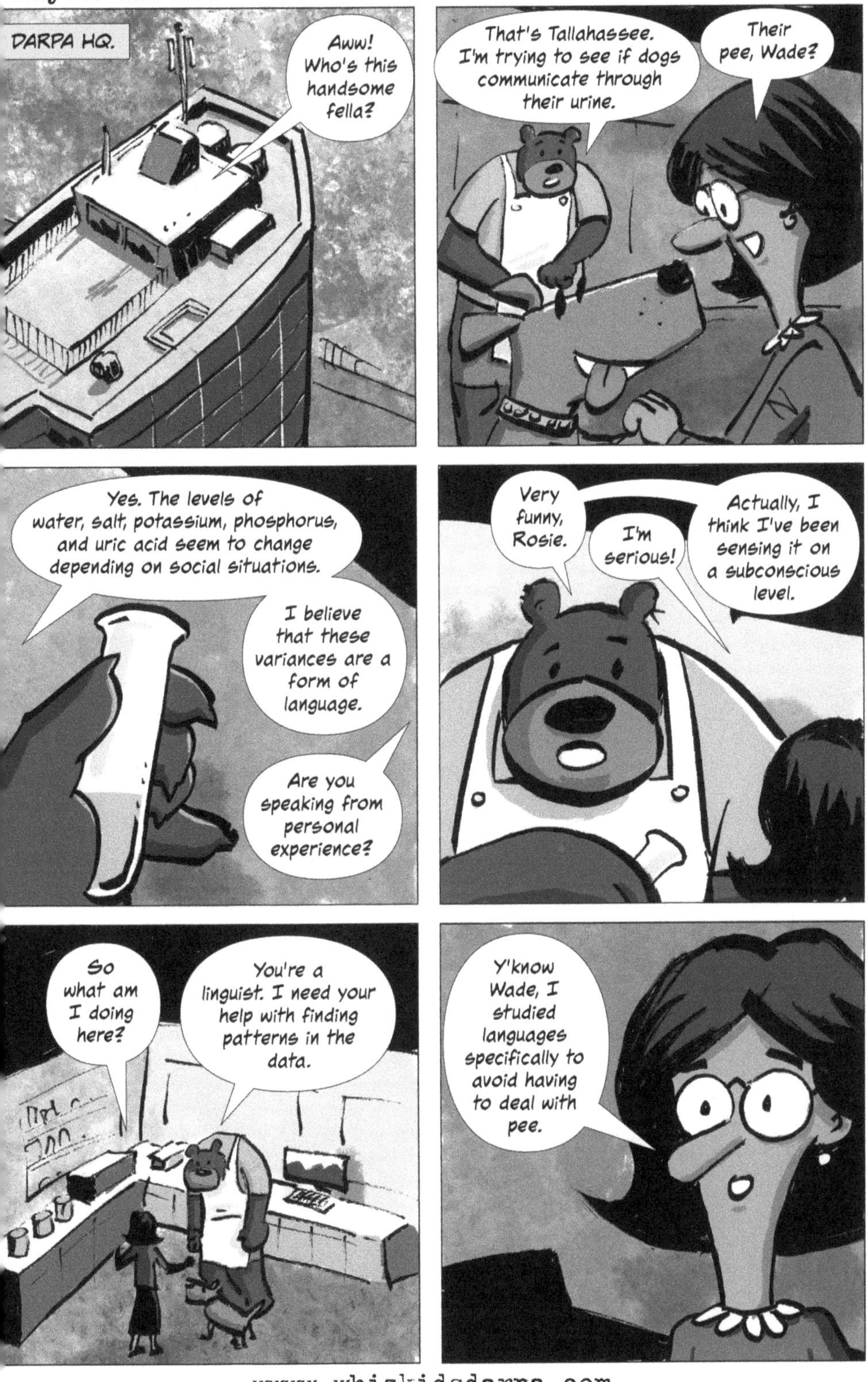
DARPA HQ.
Aww! Who's this handsome fella?
That's Tallahassee. I'm trying to see if dogs communicate through their urine.
Their pee, Wade?
Yes. The levels of water, salt, potassium, phosphorus, and uric acid seem to change depending on social situations.
I believe that these variances are a form of language.
Are you speaking from personal experience?
Very funny, Rosie.
I'm serious!
Actually, I think I've been sensing it on a subconscious level.
So what am I doing here?
You're a linguist. I need your help with finding patterns in the data.
Y'know Wade, I studied languages specifically to avoid having to deal with pee.

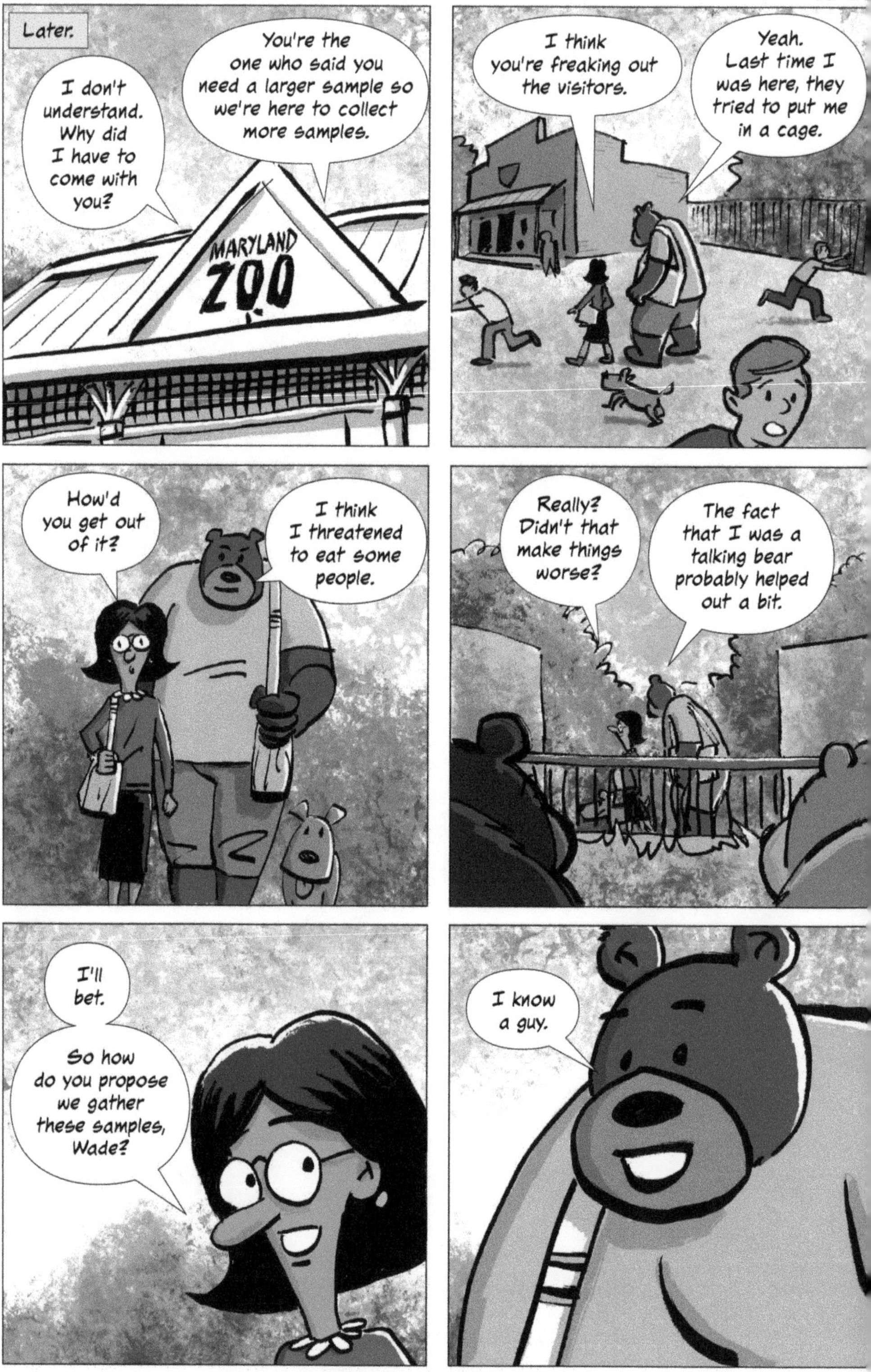
Later.
I don't understand. Why did I have to come with you?
You're the one who said you need a larger sample so we're here to collect more samples.
MARYLAND ZOO
I think you're freaking out the visitors.
Yeah. Last time I was here, they tried to put me in a cage.
How'd you get out of it?
I think I threatened to eat some people.
Really? Didn't that make things worse?
The fact that I was a talking bear probably helped out a bit.
I'll bet.
So how do you propose we gather these samples, Wade?
I know a guy.

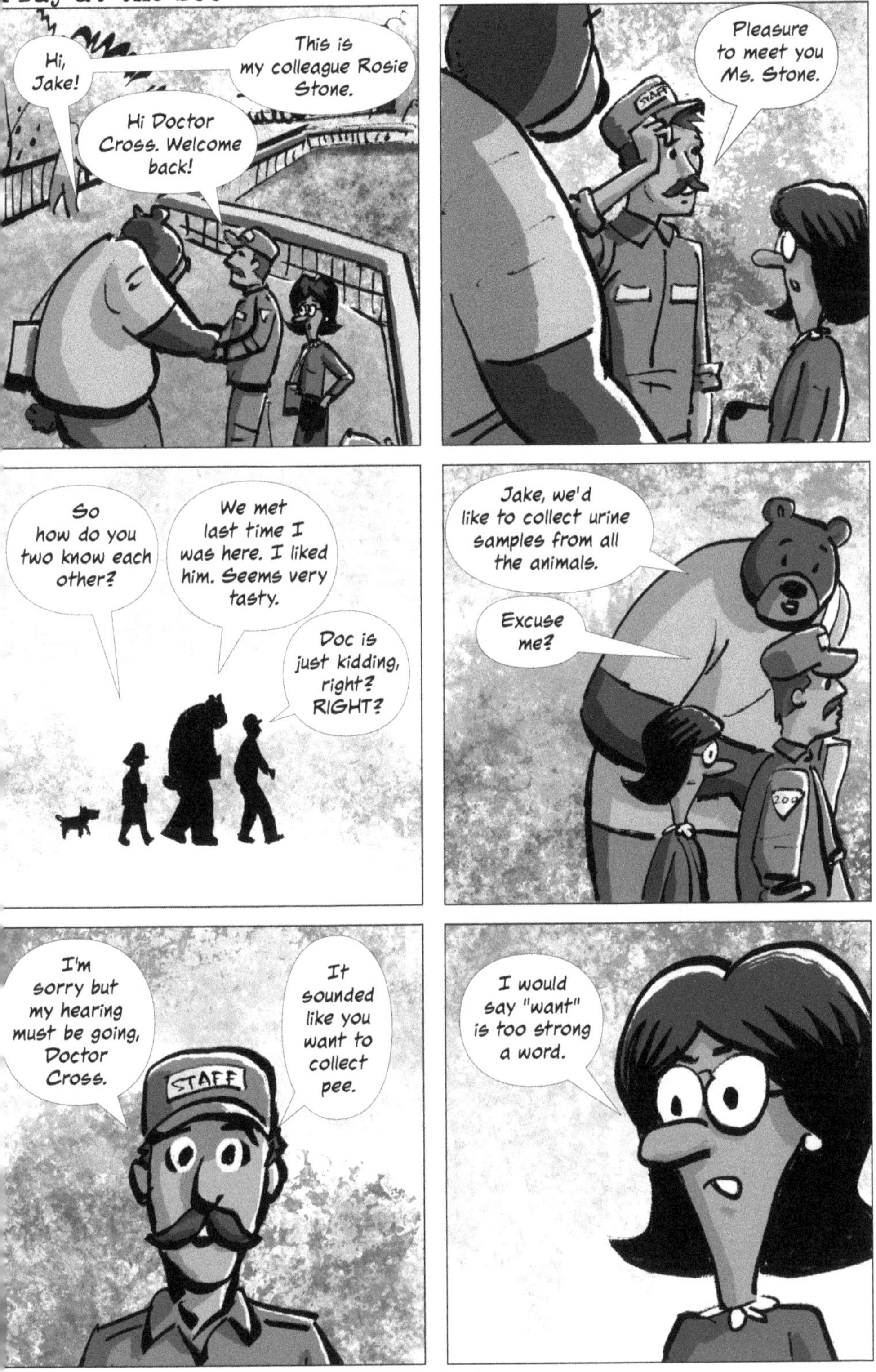
Hi, Jake!
This is my colleague Rosie Stone.
Hi Doctor Cross. Welcome back!
Pleasure to meet you Ms. Stone.
STAFF
So how do you two know each other?
We met last time I was here. I liked him. Seems very tasty.
Doc is just kidding, right? RIGHT?
Jake, we'd like to collect urine samples from all the animals.
Excuse me?
ZOO
I'm sorry but my hearing must be going, Doctor Cross.
It sounded like you want to collect pee.
STAFF
I would say "want" is too strong a word.

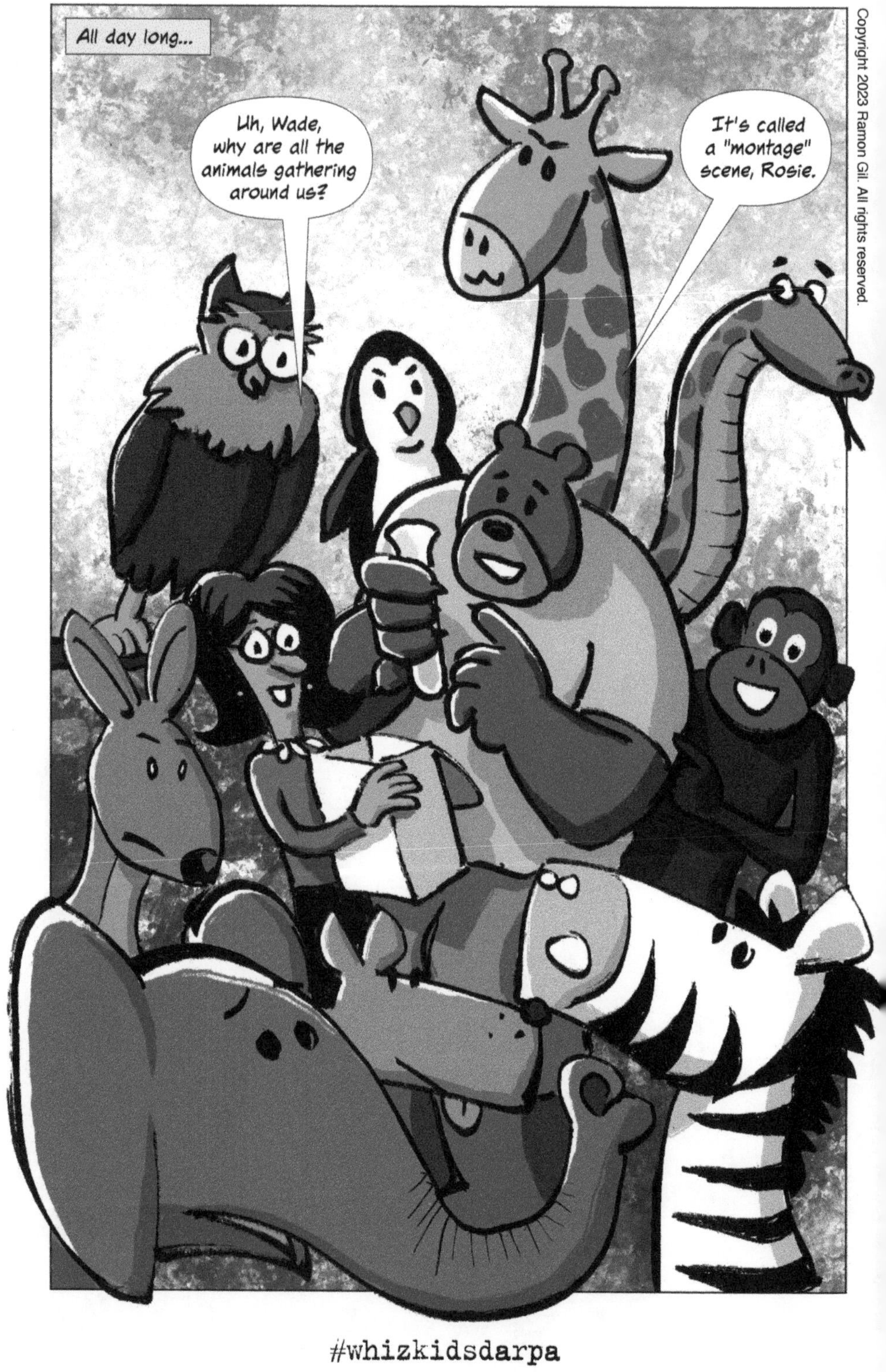
All day long...
Uh, Wade, why are all the animals gathering around us?
It's called a "montage" scene, Rosie.

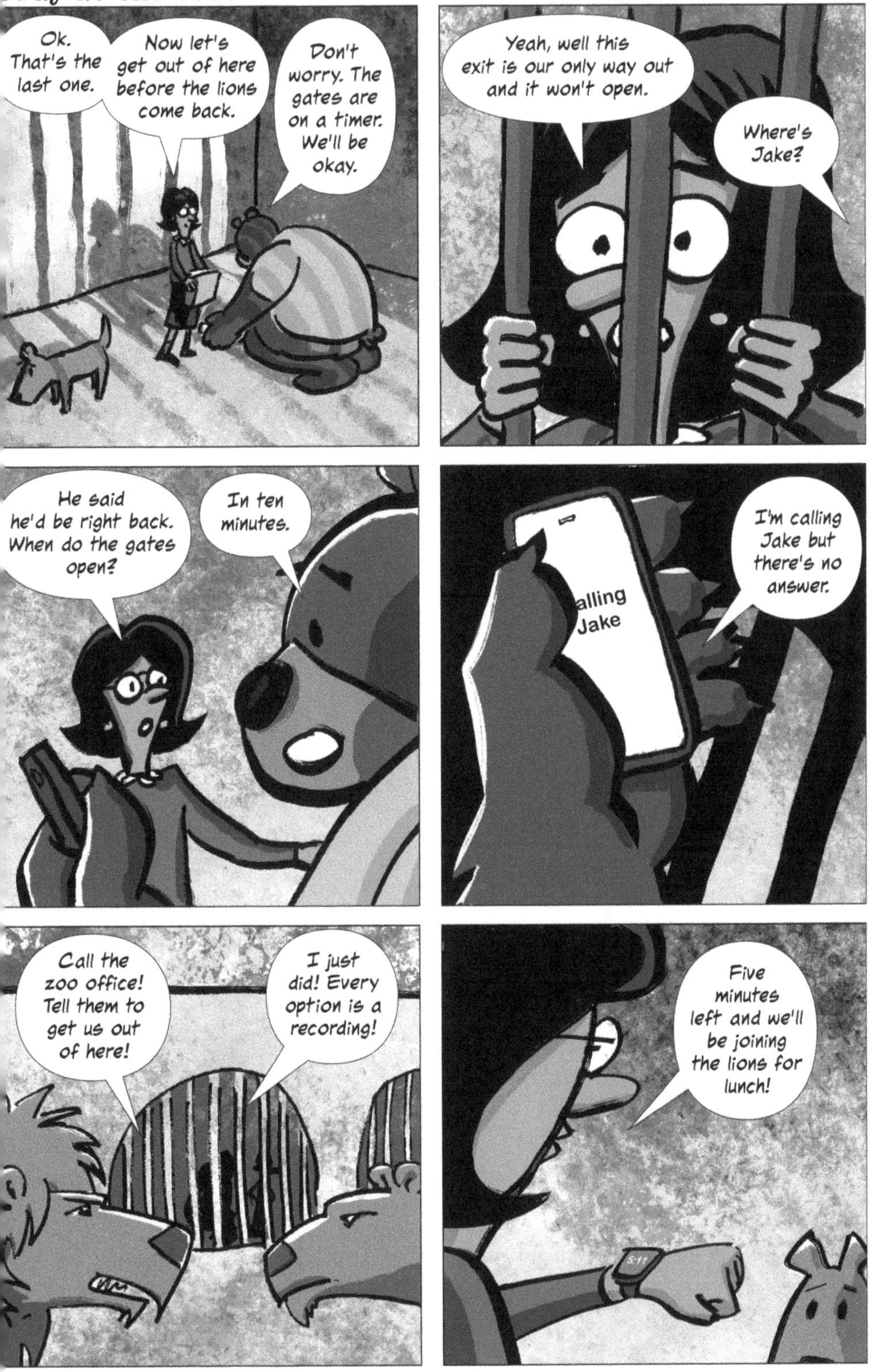
Ok. That's the last one.
Now let's get out of here before the lions come back.
Don't worry. The gates are on a timer. We'll be okay.
Yeah, well this exit is our only way out and it won't open.
Where's Jake?
He said he'd be right back. When do the gates open?
In ten minutes.
alling Jake
I'm calling Jake but there's no answer.
Call the zoo office! Tell them to get us out of here!
I just did! Every option is a recording!
Five minutes left and we'll be joining the lions for lunch!

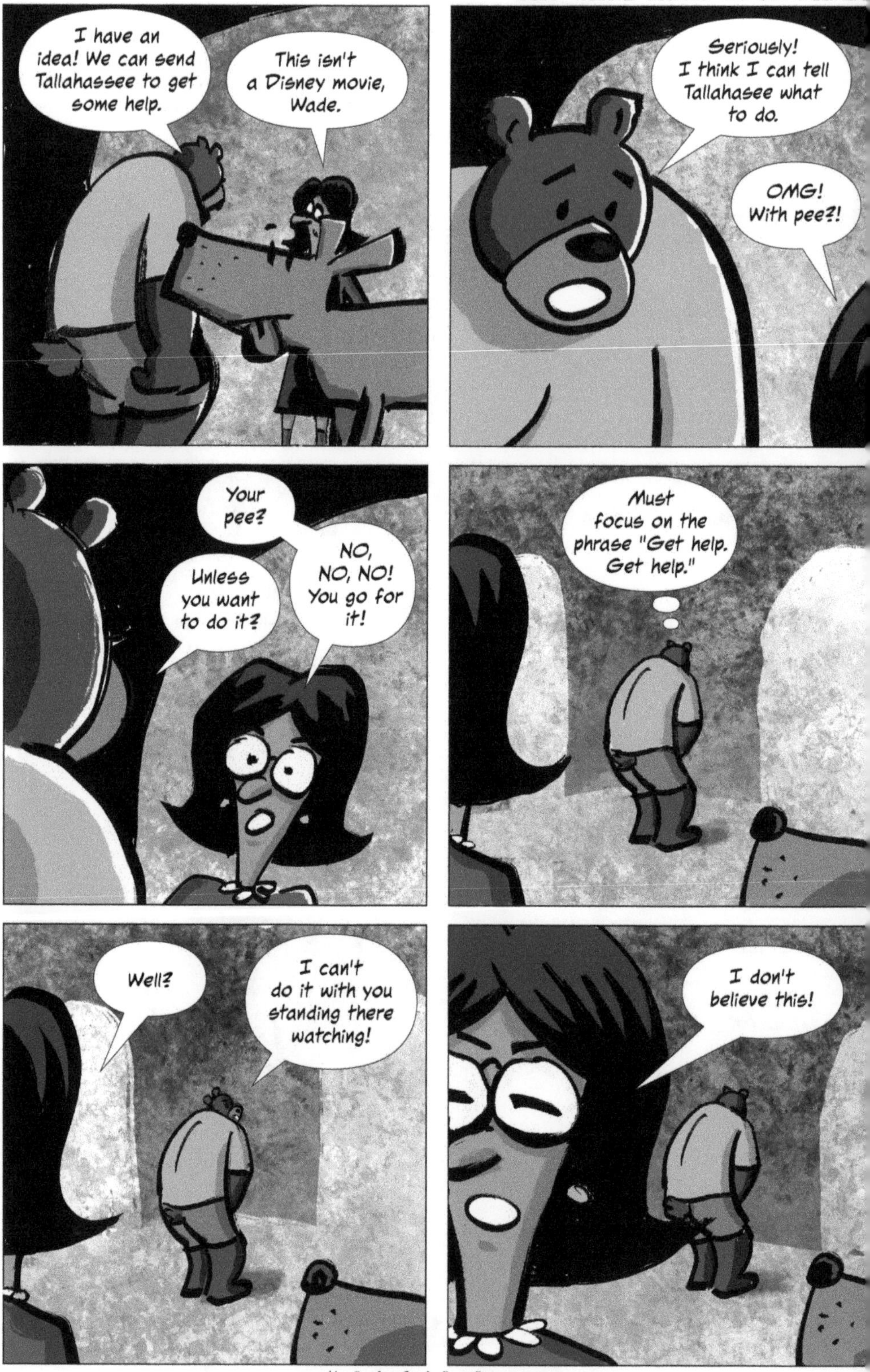
I have an idea! We can send Tallahassee to get some help.
This isn't a Disney movie, Wade.
Seriously! I think I can tell Tallahasee what to do.
OMG! With pee?!
Your pee?
Unless you want to do it?
NO, NO, NO! You go for it!
Must focus on the phrase "Get help. Get help."
Well?
I can't do it with you standing there watching!
I don't believe this!

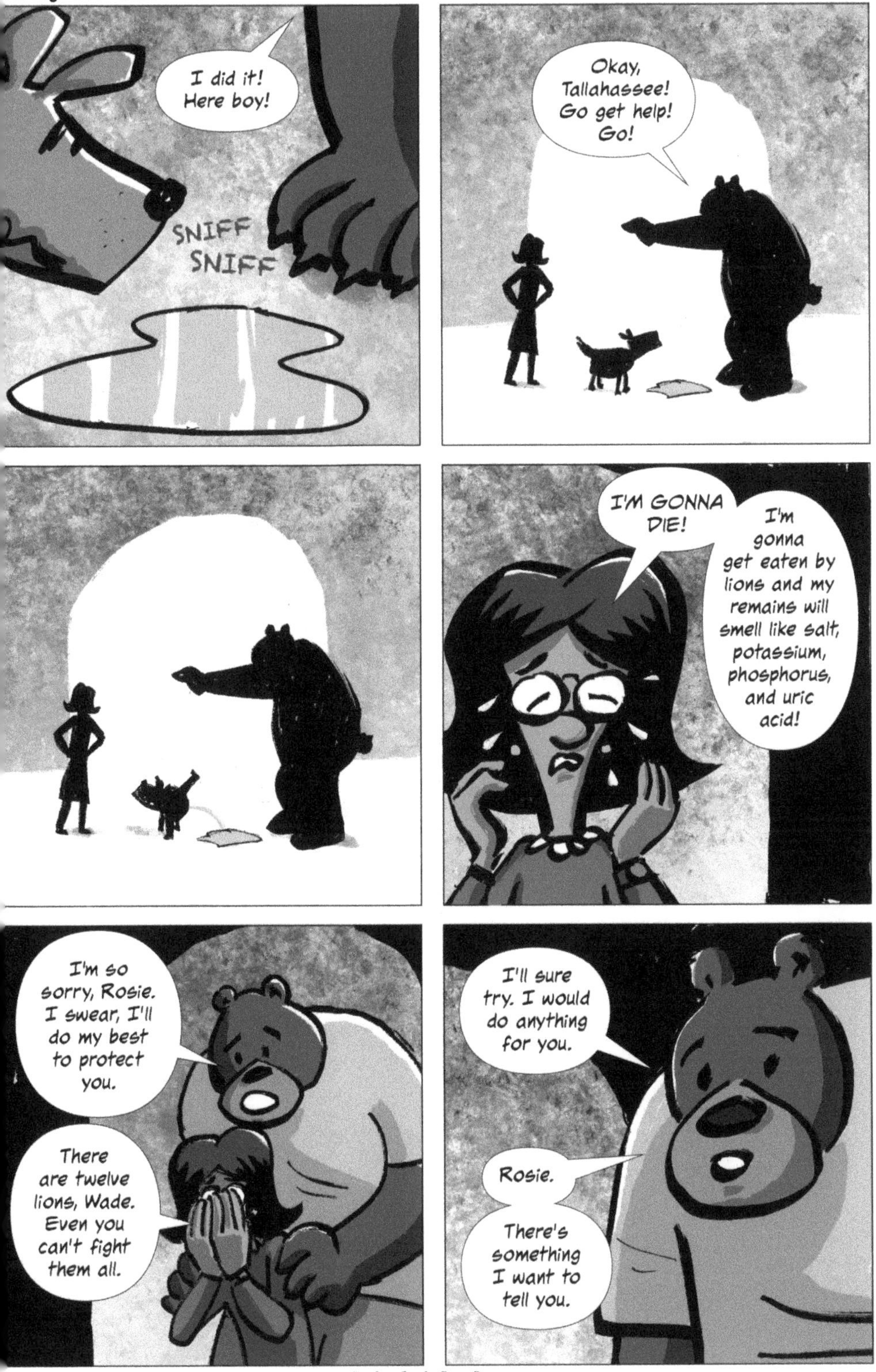
I did it! Here boy!
SNIFF SNIFF
Okay, Tallahassee! Go get help! Go!
I'M GONNA DIE!
I'm gonna get eaten by lions and my remains will smell like salt, potassium, phosphorus, and uric acid!
I'm so sorry, Rosie. I swear, I'll do my best to protect you.
There are twelve lions, Wade. Even you can't fight them all.
I'll sure try. I would do anything for you.
Rosie.
There's something I want to tell you.

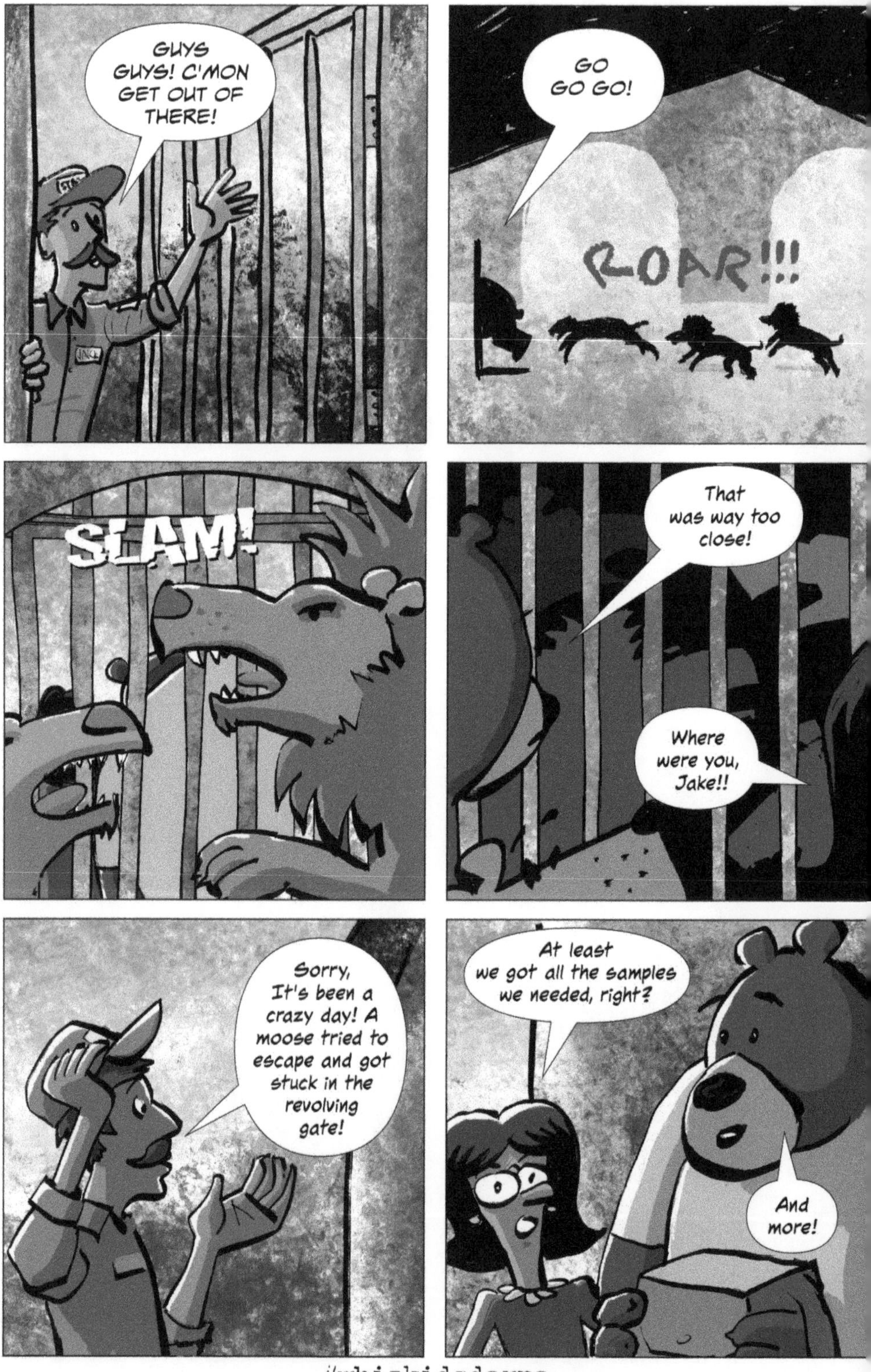
GUYS GUYS! C'MON GET OUT OF THERE!
GO GO GO!
ROAR!!!
SLAM!
That was way too close!
Where were you, Jake!!
Sorry, It's been a crazy day! A moose tried to escape and got stuck in the revolving gate!
At least we got all the samples we needed, right?
And more!

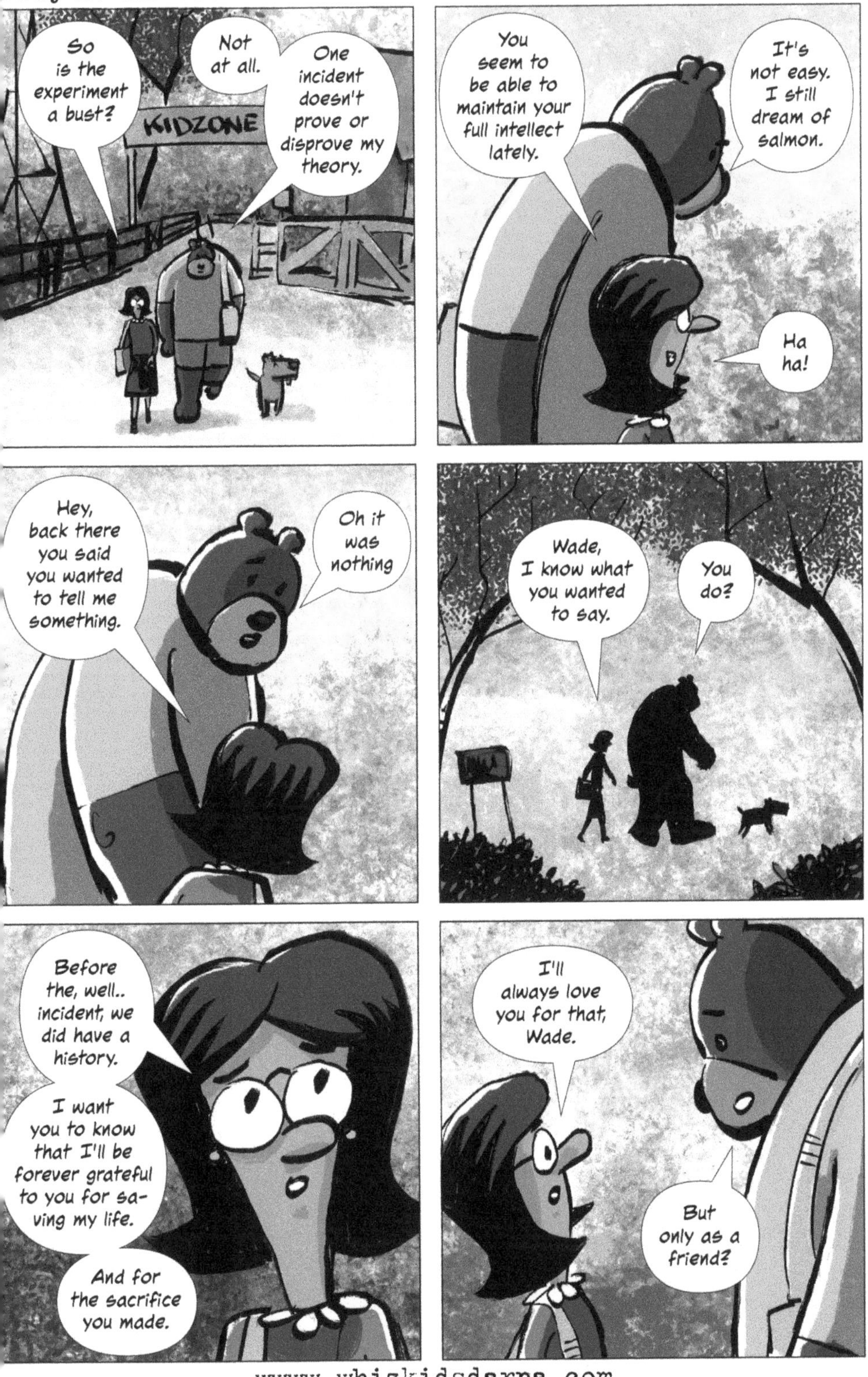
So is the experiment a bust?
KIDZONE
Not at all.
One incident doesn't prove or disprove my theory.
You seem to be able to maintain your full intellect lately.
It's not easy. I still dream of salmon.
Ha ha!
Hey, back there you said you wanted to tell me something.
Oh it was nothing
Wade, I know what you wanted to say.
You do?
Before the, well.. incident, we did have a history.
I want you to know that I'll be forever grateful to you for saving my life.
And for the sacrifice you made.
I'll always love you for that, Wade.
But only as a friend?

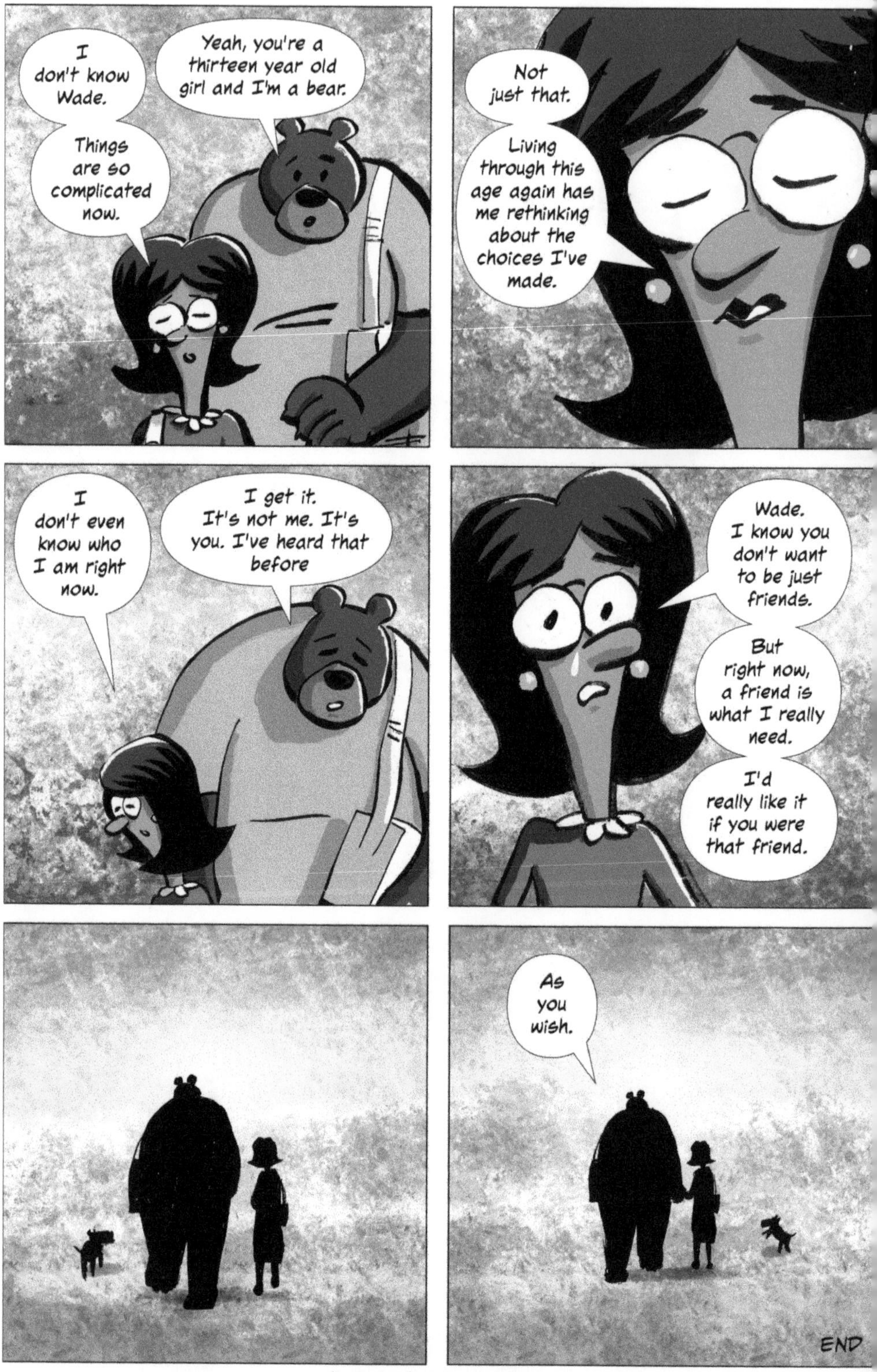
I don't know Wade.
Things are so complicated now.
Yeah, you're a thirteen year old girl and I'm a bear.
Not just that.
Living through this age again has me rethinking about the choices I've made.
I don't even know who I am right now.
I get it. It's not me. It's you. I've heard that before
Wade. I know you don't want to be just friends.
But right now, a friend is what I really need.
I'd really like it if you were that friend.
As you wish.
END

Science Check

Urine As Communication

Animals are able to use urine or pee to communicate with each other. Dogs are able to smell the hormones produced by another dog while they're urinating. With this information, dogs are able to determine each other's emotions and stress levels. Dogs also use urination to establish territory or dominance, with bigger dogs peeing higher against objects to indicate their size.

So when you take your dog out for the walk and they it seems like they are peeing EVERYWHERE, they are actually saying "Hi" to their friends maybe even "Liking" their pee messages.

Other animals communicate through pee as well. Like mice, cats and fish! Some creatures are able to communicate using pheromones.

For more information:
http://www.whizkidsdarpa.com/pee

Chapter Ten: Epilogue
Who Needs A Mother?

The Whiz Kids get some mechanical help in confronting
their greatest weakness - cleaning up their rooms.

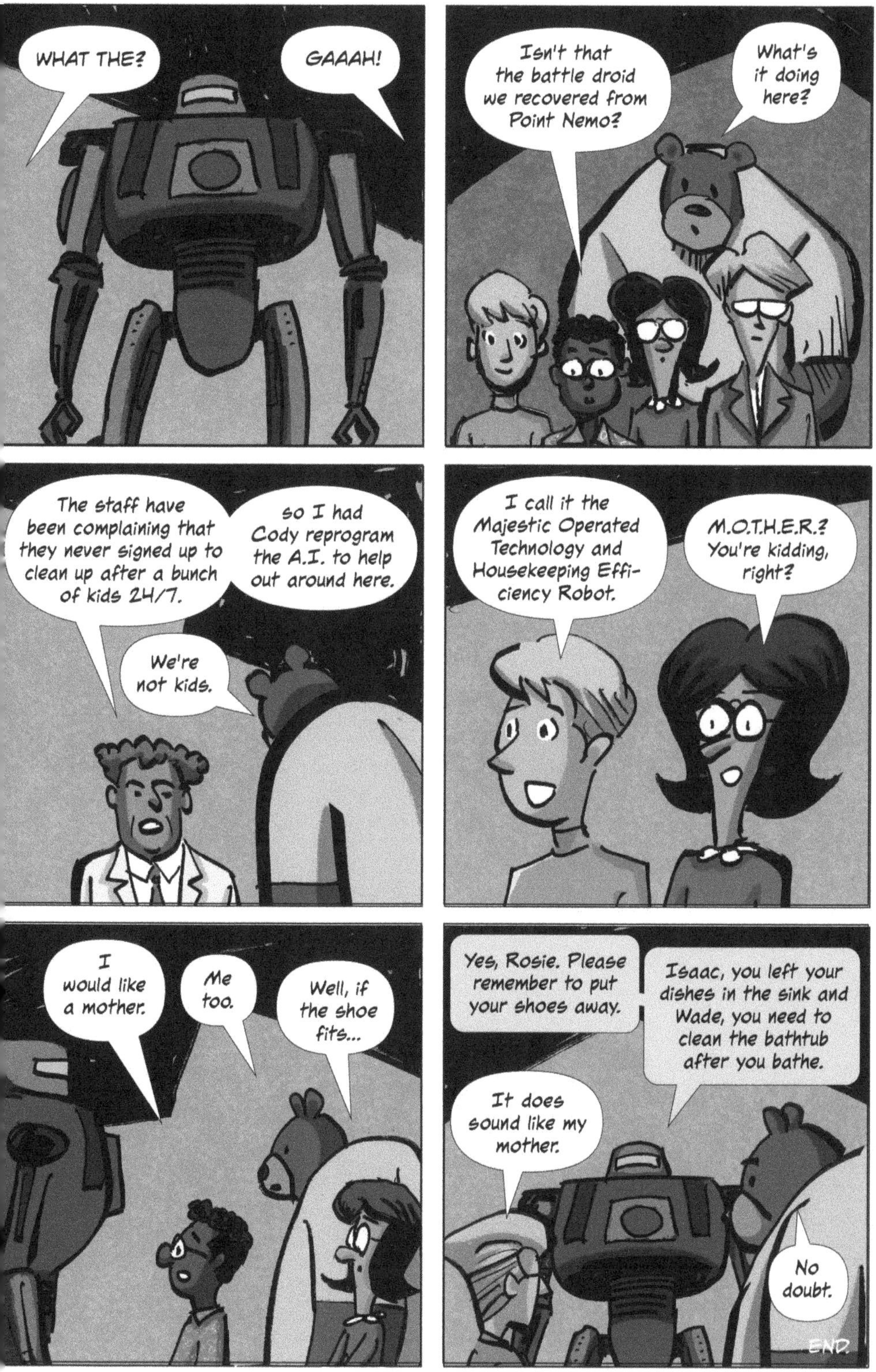
WHAT THE?
GAAAH!
Isn't that the battle droid we recovered from Point Nemo?
What's it doing here?
The staff have been complaining that they never signed up to clean up after a bunch of kids 24/7.
so I had Cody reprogram the A.I. to help out around here.
We're not kids.
I call it the Majestic Operated Technology and Housekeeping Effi-ciency Robot.
M.O.T.H.E.R.? You're kidding, right?
I would like a mother.
Me too.
Well, if the shoe fits...
Yes, Rosie. Please remember to put your shoes away.
Isaac, you left your dishes in the sink and Wade, you need to clean the bathtub after you bathe.
It does sound like my mother.
No doubt.
END.

Science Check

Artificial Intelligence

This is when you teach or program a computer to think for itself.
So that it can solve problems much more independently and even be creative. This was not possible for decades except in science fiction. But today's computers have enough calculating power and capacity to almost think like a human brain. This new advancement could mean more benefits to mankind but could also mean that machines using artificial intelligence could take over our jobs. In many science fiction stories, computers with artificial intelligence try to dominate the world.

What do you think?

 For more information:
http://www.whizkidsdarpa.com/ai

Backgrounds

The top secret files of DARPA and the team.

Isaac Juan Lee

Physicist, is the oldest of the group and the *defacto* leader as he is the clearest thinker and most level headed member. He grew up in Woodside, Queens in New York City and attended M.I.T. He joined DARPA after working for a few years at NASA. Unshakably loyal to his friends, Isaac is a fierce opponent of bullying and discrimination especially against people who are different. As a child, Isaac was diagnosed with Asperger's Syndrome but through treatment and therapy he has become quite socially adept and a capable leader.

True Age: 46
Physical Age: 13
Height: 61"
Weight: 101 lbs.
Expertise: Advanced Mathematics, Physics, Astrophysics and Quantum Theory

Cody Krilienko

Born Constantin Krilienko in Brooklyn's Brighton Beach, Cody is a computer scientist and a "warlock" level hacker, Cody is Isaac's best friend from Brooklyn Tech High School. After getting into trouble a few times with the law, Cody was recruited by the FBI but was quickly disillusioned by the work. It was at this time that Isaac brought Cody into DARPA. Cody often functions as second-in-command despite a brutally sharp and sarcastic wit.

True Age: 45
Physical Age: 12
Height: 59"
Weight: 93 lbs.
Expertise: Computer Science, Coding and Programming, Game Theory

Quentin Branch

A mechanical engineer, Quentin, hails from the
beautiful state of Hawaii. He holds several degrees
from Stanford University and Caltech where he
first attended when he was only 10 year old.
Serving as the unofficial quartermaster of the
group, Quentin is the youngest member and the
most optimistic person on the team. He is heavily
into electronic gadgets, comic books and science
fiction movies.

True Age: 39
Physical Age: 11
Height: 55"
Weight: 95 lbs.
Expertise: Engineering, Weapons, Aerospace,
Automotive Design and Industrial Fabrication

Wade Cross

A brilliant biologist and behavioral scientist, Wade's mind was trapped inside the body of an adolescent bear during the same time travel mission that caused everyone to de-age. Ironically, the most sensitive member, Wade is constantly struggling to maintain his intellect and humanity while trying to find a way to revert back to his human self. In his younger days he was also an an aspiring actor.

True Age: 42
Physical Age: 2 (in bear years)
Height: 73"
Weight: 250 lbs.
Expertise: Biology, Genetics, Behavioral Science, Psychology, Parapsychology

Rosita "Rosie" Stone

A natural linguist, Rosie is fluent in over a dozen languages. The newest member of the team and a former nemesis of the group. Rosie worked as a corporate spy, using her skills in commercial espionage but has decided to turn over a new leaf and atone for previous deeds by joining and helping her new friends. She is the most "street smart" member of the team and has a freakishly large vocabulary. Rosie can always be counted on to be a fountain of pop culture information.

True Age: 43
Physical Age: 13
Height: 59"
Weight: 85 lbs.
Expertise: Linguistics, Code Breaking, Espionage, fluent in over 12 languages

D.A.R.P.A.

Originally founded in 1958 as "ARPA", The Defense Advanced Research Projects Agency (DARPA) serves as the scientific research and development branch of the United States government. It's primary mission is to create and support the invention of applications, tools and scientific advancements for use by the intelligence community, the military and the country in general.

Among DARPA's technological contributions to the world are the computer mouse (1964), the Internet (1969), Global Positioning Satellites (GPS) tracking (1983) and Siri (2002).

Supporters

The kind folks who pledged to our Kickstarter campaign.

Teresa Adams

MarkAnthony Agbuya

Cyble Abad Alvaran

Ricki Aquino

Kathi Azim

Julie Azuma

Maria Banogon

Charlie Boatner

Matthew Buttich

Eugene Cabanban

Andrei Cabanban

Sonse Cahuni

Braddock Calumpang

Amit Chauhan

Arlene Allegre Chin

Lillian Cho

Jennie Cochran-Chinn

The Creative Fund
by BackerKit

Isaac 'Will It Work'
Dansicker

Antonio del Rosario

J. M. DeSantis

Raizanne Duell

Cheryl Duncan

Delphine & Tim Duquette

Brandon Eaker

Dr. Wayne Evans

Dwayne Farver

Catherine L. Fleming

Ophelia Gabrino

Joey Gil

Michelline Hess

Kristin Hokoyama

Albert Holaso

Brendan Hykes

Day Alfiler Ilasco

Stefan Jackson

Rally & Sherry Joaquin

Patrick Johnson

David Kawalec

Russell Kellogg

Matt Kelly

Jim Kosmicki

Kathleen Kralowec

Seymour Lavine

Lenurd the Joke Gnome

Chag Chag Leon

Deirdre Levy

Jay Lofstead

Rhodrick Magsino

Greg Maldonado

Brett Martin

Jeff Metzner

Edward Mitoma

Melvin I. Moore

Omar Morales

Yang Mou

Aaron Nickles

George O'Connor

Jesse Oberes

David Pawlan

Jill Pratzon

Emily Ree

MerienGidget Reyes

Randy Reynaldo

Nathan Rickard

Jefrey Robles

David John Rondinelli

Jon Roscetti

John R. Santos

Fabrice Sapolsky

Alexander Sapountzis

Laurie Schulz

Jonathan Señeris

John Señeris

Jason Seo

Laurence Shapiro

Nora Simpson

Josh Smith

Sasie Smittipatana

Robert J. Sodaro

Bernard Sonnie

M Sorcier

Jen the Spence

Eric Spuur

Sean Sullivan

Marta Tanrikulu

Sathya Vijayendran

Bill Walko

Debbie Wong

Kathy Wong

Sally Woo

James Yee

#whizkidsdarpa

About The Author

Ramon Gil loves tacos.

Acknowledgements

Jeric Acayen, Ester Amantiad, Julie Azuma, Moni Barette, Susan Chan, June Choi, Amy Chu, Ray De Leon, Dennis Dittrich, Gina Gagliano, Boutsaba Janetvilay, Jack Kirby, Heidi MacDonald, Mark Mazz, Ron Milon, Tyler Naimoli, Nickelodeon, Len Peralta, Pronto Comics, Cee Raymond, Fabrice Sapolsky, John Shableski

The Fashion Insitute of Technology
Masters of Fine Arts program in Illustration

My family – Glenda Villajuan, Torin and Emilio

My writing heroes – Avelina J. Gil and Gerry Gil

This book is dedicated to my late parents
Danny & Felisa Gil

wwww.whizkidsdarpa.com

Stay in Touch!

Dear readers,

I would love to hear from you! Let me know if you like this book, which parts you liked the most and which parts you didn't like. Also send me any thoughts you may have on how to make the book better!

And if you have any science story ideas, please share it. If I use your idea, I'll add your name to the "by lines"

To send me a message, just scan the code below.

Best,
Ramon Gil

Printed in the USA
CPSIA information can be obtained
at www.ICGtesting.com
CBHW040250140224
4200CB00006B/10